Notes from the Diaspora

Studies in Criticality

Shirley R. Steinberg
General Editor

Vol. 535

The Counterpoints series is part of the Peter Lang Education list.
Every volume is peer reviewed and meets
the highest quality standards for content and production.

PETER LANG
New York • Berlin • Brussels • Lausanne • Oxford

Marlon Simmons

Notes from the Diaspora

PETER LANG
New York • Berlin • Brussels • Lausanne • Oxford

Library of Congress Cataloging-in-Publication Control Number: 2022028973

Bibliographic information published by **Die Deutsche Nationalbibliothek**.
Die Deutsche Nationalbibliothek lists this publication in the "Deutsche Nationalbibliografie"; detailed bibliographic data are available on the Internet at http://dnb.d-nb.de/.

ISSN 1058-1634
ISBN 978-1-4331-9513-6 (hardcover)
ISBN 978-1-4331-9512-9 (paperback)
ISBN 978-1-4331-9510-5 (ebook pdf)
ISBN 978-1-4331-9511-2 (epub)
DOI 10.3726/b19402

© 2022 Peter Lang Publishing, Inc., New York
80 Broad Street, 5th floor, New York, NY 10004
www.peterlang.com

All rights reserved.
Reprint or reproduction, even partially, in all forms such as microfilm, xerography, microfiche, microcard, and offset strictly prohibited.

To those seeking to better the human condition

Contents

Acknowledgments   ix

   Introduction: Notes from the Diaspora   1
1. Writing Black Life: Theoretical Underpinnings   9
2. Locating Black Life within Colonial Modernity: Decolonial Notes   25
3. Politics of Urban Diasporized Youth and Possibilities for Belonging   47
4. Diaspora, Citizenry, Becoming Human and the Education of African-Canadian Youth   65
5. The Race to Modernity: Understanding Culture through the Diasporic-Self   81
6. Dialogue with Fanon   103

Acknowledgments

It has been over a decade since I first put pen to paper, or should I say, since I typed the first page which started the journey of bringing together this collection of chapters. During that time, my thoughts have shifted in many ways, more so through discussions as a graduate student at the University of Toronto, Ontario, Institute for the Studies in Education (OISE), and through my time teaching undergraduate and graduate students at the Werklund School of Education, University of Calgary. I would like to acknowledge my gratitude to Professor George Sefa Dei, Nana Adusei Sefa Tweneboah, for his mentorship and resolute support as my supervisor during my doctoral studies at OISE. Nana provided years of intellectual guidance and steadfast comradeship through my struggles and heart-warming moments. I would also like to thank the students in Nana's thesis group. Our conversations resonated with me in many ways, and will always serve as a signpost of solidarity. Thanks to Professor Shirley Steinberg for providing a pathway to publish this work, which gives voice to some of the untold stories of the Diaspora. Thank you Professor Kari Dehli for your discerning thoughts and gentle reminders about the unevenness of the writing process. To Professor Peter Trifonas, I am thankful for your earnest considerations that raised important questions for the inquiry. To my mummy, Lynette Simmons, and brother Dexter Simmons, thank you for your unbounded love, support, and belief in me. My spouse, Mairi McDermott, and children Ida and Leo Simmons, you encourage, stimulate, and provide unending care and love. These moments are dear to my heart. My nieces Brianna and Chelsea Simmons, your curiosity inspires me. My father, Reynold Simmons, your presence has always been with me. Jim and Veronica McDermott, thank you for your conversations at the dinner table which serve as a tacit prompt regarding the significance of doing this work. Liam McDermott, you remind me of the importance of laughter when thinking through these everyday historical moments.

Introduction: Notes from the Diaspora

This writing emerged from the myriad conversations I had while working through the cultural constellations of my Diasporic life. I engaged these constellations through an autoethnographic approach to make sense of my experiences of Black life as contoured through the local and the global. During the course of writing this text, my theoretical sensibilities grew in ways allowing for relational readings of my social environments. In so doing, I broached some of the limitations and possibilities involved in the process of this mind work. This text portrays my intellectual journey, filled with struggles, contradictions, and coming to make sense of my ongoing politics, which over the course of the collection has changed yet sometimes remained fixed.

Notes from the Diaspora traverses through distinct temporal periods from the late 1980s to 2020, broaching historical and contemporary tropes of Black life. Journeying through the chapters written post-2000s, I attend to a series of discussions concerning germane themes immanent to the Black experience, such as colonization, modernity, race, decoloniality, becoming and unbecoming of the human, Diaspora, and questions of belonging and citizenship. In this collection of chapters,

I draw from a range of scholars such as Frantz Fanon, Claudia Jones, Sylvia Wynter, C. L. R. James, and W. E. B. Du Bois, among other social theorists to situate intellectual discussions regarding Diasporic communities. The articles are primarily concerned with the ways in which Diasporic people make sense of their experiences within their contemporary society through transoceanic histories, and simultaneously how they come to reimagine and construct different ways of being human as shaped through particular enactments of self-determination. The chapters uncover the variant interests, present epistemological challenges, and historical issues about my Diasporic life, by dialoguing with the present within historical instantiations of modernity and colonization. The discussions take up the different ways of presenting current challenges for Diasporic social formations, the interplay of cultural tradition and modernity, contestations over knowledge production, and the roles and significance of local cultural resource knowledge for thinking about Diasporic life in its varied representations. Other related discussions include social stratification, inequality, and questions of identity.

Notes from the Diaspora gives pathways to make sense of how particular beliefs, values, attitudes, and politics come to be embedded within histories of colonial discourses. Further, it points to decolonial thought as necessary for the formation of different social imaginaries as shaped through epistemological Diasporas. Discursive regularities and irregularities are broached to draw on sensibilities concerned with quotidian expressions and taken-for-granted understandings immanent to historical and current Diasporic temporalities. *Notes from the Diaspora* considers some of the terms and conditions for Diasporic participation and detachment, to denote how particular communicative exchanges become rendered within social practices. Such a Diasporic account allows for the placement of historical trajectories onto the innumerable experiences as delimited to the present, while concomitantly having strategies to cogently read into the discursive sociomaterial properties of the present. The collection of chapters here attend to the social histories often displaced by way of colonial endowments of institutionalized knowledge.

Diaspora is at once a sequencing of histories, one which inaugurates relatedness to the present, making new relations and ways of knowing that diverge and converge from historical Enlightenment socializing practices. The African Diaspora has endured a long colonial history. Since colonization, the growth of Diasporic thought has been entangled with epistemological relations, which have had to live up to the task of understanding the movement of people through the concomitant sociomaterial production of modernity. Though these relations are sometimes incommensurable, one of the key claims of Diasporic thought is with encapsulating the frequencies in which the present is involved with comprehending conditional temporalities as ensconced within complex diachronic routes of coloniality.

With this conceptualization in mind, Diasporic thought has continued to open debates and questions about the complexities of existing social realities, which often have been over-determined through theoretical analysis that leans toward commensurable, rational, and linear outcomes as the only valid way of knowing. While Diasporic thought draws from historical accounts of social theory, many of the theorists situate their thinking in ways that epistemologically diverge and converge from them. Offering such an account allows for compound ruptures of historical and, specifically, institutionalized theoretical claims. What ensued with this rupture is a repositioning of deliberations that have been tangentially placed regarding discussions about modernity, giving rise to a mode of thinking steeped in a genealogy that temporally uproots colonial epistemologies. I am less interested in suggesting Diasporic thought remains ahistorical to social theory or providing a sum fixed definition of Diasporic thought that unwittingly could bring epistemological closure to the field. Rather, I am concerned with writing Diasporic thought through a language that offers the public different entry points to reconcile with histories of systems of thought that have worked their way within the hegemonic scaffolding of academe. In this respect, a methodological approach ought to involve transoceanic sifting of archival notes, obligatory points of passage, memory, quotidian experiences, situated ethics, and diachronic relations. Such an approach reopens past and present in a dialectical manner, in so far as within the social science field of educational research, the impact of Diasporic thought has both been direct and simultaneously enacted from multiple viewpoints. To note here, Diasporic thought shouldered a set of epistemological dislodgment regarding meaning-making sensibilities within the sociology of knowledge. This dislodgement worked as a disentangling practice, where normalized ways of knowing were questioned, entrenched habits governed within institutions as ensconced within the conduits of power and knowledge were made salient, and through the continuity of care regarding the ethic of the Diasporic-self as a scholar.

In its epistemological journey, Diasporic thought has become sort of a criterion for scholars working in educational research pursuing epistemological questions around belonging, citizenship, identity, colonization, racism, oppression, qualitative inquiry, and ethical concerns involved with teaching and learning. This epistemological journey ought not to be limited to scholarly writing, which in a totalizing way subverted colonial ways of knowing. Concomitant and immanent to Diasporic epistemes are a series of activism works that have been built over histories of colonial resistance. These subversive encounters have shaped Diaspora and emerging writings, and offer innovative ways to contribute as political actors in contemporary globalized societies. Writing through these experiences discursively and sociomaterially allows for an overhaul and renewal of Diasporic histories. In turn, *Notes from the Diaspora* questions those histories that govern origin narratives of the nation-state, colonial representations of citizenship, and what constitutes the preferred subject. The questioning then influences a form of provocation that pushes public and institutionalized understandings of given epistemological relations which have been temporally steeped through past and present histories, culminating in social imaginaries being enacted as outside the colonial encounter. What *Notes form the Diaspora* sets in place is an active interruption of colonial knowledge systems through the congeries of inter- and intra-geographies and histories with the propensity to situate the present relationally with the past. This interruption is set in place by way of a series of conceptualizations, which moves across a range of intellectual traditions, methodological approaches, and reflections, fecundating theoretical sensibilities necessary for writing Diaspora as enmeshed within historical and ongoing social realities. Such an approach allows for heuristic engagements to comprehend contingent sociomaterial relations, desires, and potentialities of those enactments and relations latent within the epistemic constellations of the Diaspora. Made anew are approaches to continue the journey of qualitative methodologies that aptly attend to histories of cultural difference and resulting meaning-making possibilities, at the same time working to delimit obsolescent readings of the past as sedimentary within the present. Writing Diaspora in this way directs a reading of history that makes intelligible potentials, which can generate non-hegemonic discourses, necessary for thinking about social inquiry.

The study of the Diaspora has provided incommensurable contributions to change how we understand our social and economic realities. There are also numerous studies in the fields of Education, Social Science, and the Humanities, which continue to draw from the Diaspora. These fields of study nurture a social theory with a disposition to prioritize discussions about the epistemological encumbering installed through colonial narratives embedded and entangled within the historic and present-day fabric of the governing public sphere. What, in a sense, *Notes from the Diaspora* attends to is an intellectual practice, which interrupts the 'Truth' of history. This interruption stems from theoretical underpinnings, resistance, and activist ways of becoming, all buttressed in an ontology temporally reified through the interstices of geographies, histories, place, culture, and a particular peopling which have formed itself through sequences of changing and unchanging events. At the heart of my concern is figuring out how the Diasporic-self is formed, and through what ontological terms and epistemological conditions the Diasporic-self becomes governed under the inscription of particular ethical codes of conduct. With this writing project, the foci are on the threads of history constitutive of ethical relations with the self and ensuing practices of self-governance undertaken within the ongoing political specificities of one's social reality. Colonial entrapment, perils, desires, dangers, and pleasures are queried to seek how they become enacted under practices from the Diaspora as governed by present-day ethics. What ethical modes are made possible to put into place the making of the Diasporic-self? And what techniques and instruments are relied upon for the forming of self in such ways?

Notes from the Diaspora cares about how social processes establish themselves in relational configurations of power and knowledge through deliberate endeavors at nurturing belonging, becoming, self-determination, resistance, and ethical practices of the self to cast different social arrangements necessary to form a transformative society. This journey is situated by way of a social theory, one absorbed and made durable through forms of thinking with foci on reflections and memory, generative of establishing historical problems of the nation-state as constituted through the governance of the self, and relations with a difference as organized through the entangled power apparatus of the state. The purpose then involves doing the mind work to come up with different questions pertaining to history in relation to the variant perspectives of colonial histories, which have come to script present life. These questions then, in turn, can link themes of belonging through ethical cartographies of caring and loving the Diasporic-self within the framework of unfolding Diasporic practices, to the extent of broaching how these practices are made intelligible can also be addressed.

Such an approach is inextricably linked to histories of citizenship, colonial politics of representation, and universalized and particular configurations of what it means to be human as self-determining people within a political foray respective to nation-state edicts. Building on this line of thinking, *Notes from the Diaspora* is concerned about experiences of belonging as constituted through the concomitant presence of Diasporic sensibilities, which in effect resulted from different activities of resistance, nurturing in the process, and relations cognizant of how pre-determining colonial histories condition wellness of Black life. Another approach this collection of chapters takes up is with tending to the relations of the Diasporic-self as fostered through decolonial thought and how in turn these relations navigate the present terms and conditions of globalization. I have drawn on these sensibilities throughout the chapters to bring attention to Black Diasporic people as situated in particular nation-states to make salient the current theoretical significance regarding how they come to govern the self under the edicts of the state. I am suggesting in the field of social theory, the study of social realities as constituted through the Diaspora allows for the consideration of ethical practices steeped within the myriad politics of the Diasporized-self. In that, ethics and politics of the self as yielded through reflexivity is increasingly contingent on relationships formed through subversive modes of knowledge transformative of rethinking one's history as a decolonial practice.

Notes from the Diaspora is asking how histories of Black life can offer modes of thinking necessary to subvert historical formations of colonial epistemologies. It challenges the problem of universalized purist approaches to life and contends with the resulting effects of knowing and positioning of Black people and their social realities within the racial classifications of their communities.

Marlon Simmons
April 12, 2022
Calgary

1.

Writing Black Life: Theoretical Underpinnings

Introduction

Though Black communities have been in Canada for centuries, their experiences as citizens have been slowly becoming better. From being underpaid, to unemployment, to credential devaluation, and to perennial housing discrimination, Black communities continue to face substantial challenges integrating into the civic and economic life of Canada. What is needed are different ways of interpreting Canadian citizenry, which could inform their human rights, build transformative practices for educational policies, and critically inform leadership practices for Black youth as well as the broader context of Canadian communities. One of the foci here is to theoretically trace the untold social formations of Black life to understand how these different cultures engage intergenerational knowledge and cultural memory of the past and present to deal with the challenges of a globalized world in the context of Canada. I address the complex dynamics of how diverse Black communities come to situate their place of belonging within respective Canadian societies. The aim is to provide an alternative means of understanding how Black life experiences different forms of belonging through particular cultural understandings embedded within the African Diaspora. I conceptualize Black life through particular encoded discursive fields with historical specificities to colonization and plantation life that locate the sociomaterial on African peoples. In this discussion, I tend to the sociomateriality of Blackness by thinking through variant histories of Black life. Though these histories speak to the relational experiences of Black life, of movement—wittingly or unwittingly—the concern here is with how Black life becomes positioned within the nation-state and what sorts of becoming are made possible. These experiences cannot be denied historically. As such, the intention is with extricating Black ontologies as embodied within the land and Black life, to situate Black histories as unfolding within the nation-state and the ensuing text, rather than always already tangential.

Let me say a bit about how I am working to conceptualize these everyday moments experienced in Black life. I am interested in the variant modes and procedures of Black social formations in which Black peoples come to know and govern the self through particular identifications and popularized social media desires which materialize in an everyday performative or ritualized practice. I am curious about how particular Black social formations come to accept these identifications as being performed through a constellation of histories as a continuity. My interest is in knowing how race and culture concomitantly produce performative desires that form the conditions of existence for Black life. I am thinking of Black life through innumerable material embodiments of time and space and socio-historic-cultural processes as interwoven by way of difference immanent to Black cultures as shaped through the uncertainty of the Diasporic movement. I am writing to ease the tension of a historical, homogenous, singular, and immutable read on Black life. Yet, as a method, writing through the Diaspora presents complexities. With its shifting terrains, contoured historically through different sociocultural enactments, the Diaspora, as configured through the local and the global, materializes through uncertainty in ways in which Black life and its ensuing relationship with its social world speak to the infinitude of possibilities of what it means to be human (Mignolo, 2015; Wynter, 2003; Walcott, 2003). I am intrigued more so by the way in which Black life has become autonomous through the continuous absorption and withdrawal of local stories, traditional narratives, which inevitably come to propel the ordering of thought, the sociality, and the peopling as imbued through the transferring of ideas as embodied within Diasporic relations.

Black Life

With Blackness, my foci involve understanding the ways in which meanings of Black life have been discursively and materially constituted and how such meanings are made anew in its contemporaneity. In so doing, and as a method of social inquiry, I draw from raw materials such as Blackness, race, relationships with the land, Indigeneity, nation-state governmentality as conditioned through colonial modernity, and immigration policies constitutive of the nation-building initiative in Canada. Black life gives us a place to think of historic specificities of expropriation of Indigenous lands, racism, Diaspora, white supremacy, African enslavement, and the project of settler nation-state. Through its anachronistic temporality as conditioned by way of colonial forays, Black life became organized, regulated, and recognized through the governing sociomaterial techniques of colonial power. Black life provides the social and material practices necessary for creating imaginative directions that can help with refashioning the historical work of writing difference and belonging. Such writing congeals through epistemological Diasporas as embodied through African enslavement and made wholesome by quotidian events that are actually linked through time and place to current issues and a particular past.

We know Black life is deeply embedded within colonial enslavement of African peoples, that it concerns a way of thinking that orients itself through resistance, struggle, and social justice (Fanon, 1963). With Black life, I am thinking about the sociopolitical thought experienced among African peoples concerning the human condition of post-plantation life. In a sense, I am taking up Black life as an approach to understand how Diasporic-African peoples worked through the imperial contours of the contested terrain of sovereignty. I am thinking of Black life as temporal, as an anachronistic interruption to colonial governance, which situates through space and time, liminal Diasporic sensibilities that integrate Black life by way of contrapuntal pedagogies. I am suggesting that writing and reading Black life involve Diasporic enactments, which holistically speak to the history, culture, and spirituality of African peoples. I would imagine then that Diaspora invites inclusivity amid historical classifications of Euro-colonial modernity and Black life.

Of particular interest to Black life is the economic and social movement of peoples to Canada. Often enough this movement has been one dimensional, from archipelagos historically steeped in colonial manacles to harvesting territories that reap the materials of enslavement. This movement has also been enacted in ways that promulgated unbelonging for Blackness, as outside what it means to be a citizen and engage in civic participation as governed within the prescripts of a self-identifying democratic nation-state. Nested within this movement are troubles immanent to colonial-settler governance that saw educational systems, finance economies, and jobs being difficult terrains to navigate for Black peoples. Public sphere conversations concerning Black life have come under discursive surveillance (Browne, 2015), in which Black life comes to be articulated and sociomaterially represented in ways that place their positionality as secondary within the history of the colonial nation-state. Indeed, the constitutive makeup of the nation-state is deeply entrenched within colonial violence. Consequently, as the nation-state renews itself through imperial space and time, belonging for Black life continues to be positioned and marked through colonial inscriptions. With this in mind, I am seeking to write Black life beyond the parochial conduits that repeatedly shape Blackness through devalued forms of citizenry. In so doing, I want to have a conversation that speaks to the experience of Diasporic-African peoples, in the context of being transnationally located. I want to trouble the ways in which these transhistorical experiences have been framed through particular theoretical frameworks. I am asking how might we begin to understand questions of what it means to belong for Black life when historically belonging becomes ontologically contrapuntal and coterminously situated to the human archetype. An understanding that dialectically speaks to the experience of belonging, through historical acts of movements. As a starting point, I want to consider how Black life, as located within the Americas emerging from Africa through Civil Rights encounters, comes into personhood through the unfreedoms of emancipation. In a sense, I am thinking about how Blackness comes to understand the variant terms and conditions of belonging through different articulations of the African Diaspora.

If, and as Hall (2007) reminds us, immanent to the self are histories of the past, then much of Black life involves working through the materiality of these narratives to get a sense of how synergies of the past and present come into discursive and material enactments in particular public spheres such as schools, job settings, community building, friendships, family relations, and just civic participation. Circumscribing these synergies of Black life are contingencies of globalization that mitigate Diasporic life. Understanding Black life in the context of self, difference, and sociocultural environments involves some mind-work with specific questions cognizant of histories in the global context of coloniality and the attendant modernity. The study of Black life involves a host of methods and techniques, which have congealed into a discipline. Black life has become a place where scholars, students, activists, community, and family members can draw from to make sense of, or extend upon, the literature. With this approach, Black life is less interested in being reduced to one fixed thing, but more so Black life is made durable through the different embodied practices and relational experiences.

You might ask, what constitutes Black life in its distinctive forms? What are the ways in which the study of Black life becomes a field of knowledge, institutionalized and at the same time forming epistemological modes of inclusion and exclusion within academe? After all, the study of Black life concerns understanding human practices, understanding human relations within the broader ecological sphere. What then are the ways in which the study of Black life diverges and converges from other schools of thought? And how do these diverging and converging pathways relate to the broader political relations of the world? These epistemic moments need not be neatly bound into some even compartmentalized moment as if human relations were evenly fashioned. Black life like other socialites has its own ontologies with specific characteristics and sensibilities as imbued through certain historical conditions. If one of our aims is with understanding how the relational experiences of Black life come to be consolidated through particular engagements with their broader or let us say Diasporic world, one could imagine then, that these narratives concern moments of resistance, survival, and self-determination as contingent to plantation struggles and embodied within Black life (McKittrick 2006). I am suggesting Black life is contextually bound to the conditions in which it emerged. With the foci being material change, one of the aims is to make sense of how Black life comes into the means of this materiality when the starting point in a sense becomes the self.

For Black life to have to attend to the colonial, political, and economic organizing practices of employment, it involves deciphering public sphere institutional alignments, as well as designing particular ways of knowing that correlate to the past through public memory which mitigates the present in its immediacy. I am asking then, how does Black life as interwoven with coloniality and Diasporic histories come to share ways of living with themselves as well as with other communities (Simmons & Dei, 2012)? What are the ways in which Black life learns about the conditions in which they acquire their reality? If the concern then is about how Black life makes meaning of the conditions of their reality, then part of this project is with tracing what counts as knowledge when making intelligible the crystallization processes immanent to their ensuing sociocultural register.

Perhaps we should discuss some of the underlying assumptions regarding how we are thinking of Black life. What I am working through is the domain of transmissions that enable Black life with distinctive sensibilities as situated within particular sociocultural networks, institutions, organizations, and community establishments, conveying bearings, generative of synergies in the quest for solidarity through social memory. As Black life traverses through the different pathways of globalization, the ongoing route, in due course, sifts through historical modes of thought when socializing in their everyday life. At times depending on how Black life is situated, it then becomes experienced through discontinuous histories or temporalities proving to be delayed or latent growth, not yet materializing into actualizing the self.

Mbembe's Critique of Black Reason

Achille Mbembe's compelling account in, *Critique of Black Reason* (2017), situates a re-reading of Black life through the historical contours of colonization, race, capitalism, and modernity. His underlying concern is with understanding what it means to be human through historical codifications of Black life. Weaving entwined narratives of the Black experience as anchored within complex contact zones of Africa, apartheid, the Caribbean, America, and Europe, Mbembe provides signifiers and notes from the African Diaspora to signal the importance of linking plantation sensibilities in making sense of the enslavement of African peoples, the ensuing commodification of blackness and simultaneous socioeconomic material production of Europe. With this discursive material making of Europe, Mbembe points to the stitching of colonial boundaries, which places black peoples outside, as external to Europe. He amplifies how the colonial boundaries of modernity work to govern the institutional process of the unplaceability of Black peoples, of unbelonging; in a sense, it speaks to the reification of Blackness into nonhuman entities. Attendant to this unplaceability, Mbembe points to the colonial affect imbued through the psychosocial insertions of colonization. His writing is less interested in some linear narrative of history, which provides cohesion to the coloniality of African peoples. Instead, he writes to uncover the entangled geographies of Black life as encumbered through indeterminate histories of racial classifications, cultural aesthetic practices, religion, language, and literature.

Mbembe is also thoughtful about the means of knowledge production and how these modes of relations allow for a re-identification of Black life within colonial logics. He leaves us thinking of how these terms and conditions of coloniality are made recognizable in ways that endow Black life with sociocultural practices as being contained within colonial conduits, yet at the same time moving beyond the boundaries of colonial logic. Through these historical trajectories, Mbembe presents particular sensibilities for Black reason—sensibilities that allow for different embodiments, the constellation of voices, Enlightenment discourses, intergenerational knowledge, and shared consciousness of Blackness. Sensibilities which make anew enactments immanent to everyday negotiations necessary for the self-determination of Black peoples as experienced within the globalized forays of modernity. Given the ethical proximity of essentializing Blackness, Mbembe invokes Blackness to historically dialogue with Europe's duplicitous conception of Man and Blackness as nonhuman. He leaves us thinking about the set of epistemic-material practices wherein Blackness is made fungible in ways that promulgate colonial logics. Blackness becomes desired and made abject through an interchangeable performative making permissible belonging and unbelonging of the human. In tacit ways, Mbembe notes how fungible as concomitant to market interests becomes surreptitiously steeped within practices of militarization, privatization, and digital technologies.

Across these layered textual readings of Blackness, Mbembe's work is rife with the language of the *Black Man*. One is left wondering about the myriad ways in which Blackness becomes constituted through gender and Euromodernity. How might such gendered reasoning of Blackness and modernity make intelligible *Black reason*? And how might such reason help with offering different possibilities for Black life? What we are left to work through is the elision of the Black subject as configured through the said Western consciousness. At the same time, we are pushed to think that counterhegemonic to this elision of Blackness resides anti-colonial critique. As such, this anti-colonial way of being provides *reservoirs of life* necessary for understanding what it means to be human in the global context of eco-planeterization. African enslavement, colonization, and apartheid are three events Mbembe recalls as bringing foreclosure to Black discourses. For Black subjects the resultant effects are social death and alienation of the self. Governing these historical events are the auspices of memory and religion concomitantly infused through the politics of representation as constituted through ahistorical synchronic readings of Black life. With *Critique of Black Reason*, Achille Mbembe offers futures for humanism through carefully retrieving genealogies of unmapped archives of Black life.

Linking the material of Blackness through racism and the histories of capitalism, Mbembe journeys through the historical consciousness of Black life to unearth what he calls the *reservoirs of life*. In marking these reservoirs as embodied by Black reason, Mbembe does well to identify possibilities for Black reason as such possibilities co-identify with racial classifications and stern organizing principles of life that suggest different ways of thinking about the social and the political.

History, Place, and Black Life

What it means to be human is constantly being reconfigured through different forms of belonging. How might Black life help one with understanding these shifting modes of sociality? Let us think of Black life and the history of the movement as archived through Black memory. Thinking of Black life as emerging through anti-black racism, survival, resistance, and modes of self-determination calls for remembering through histories of textual and public erasure. The movement of African peoples globally gave rise to social, material, economic, and political implications regarding historical questions of belonging and sovereignty, as these moments were embodied and constituted through the land. Black peoples are filled with a difference and possess a unique history. Sometimes these distinctive histories provide possibilities, sometimes they prove to be a limiting factor as these linguistic, religious, spiritual, cultural, gendered, ethnic, and national constructs bind with or against themselves to form cohesions or tensions that act in ways to form global markers. Understanding how Black peoples traverse these sociomaterial places in ways that strategically distance themselves, de-race, or make anew social networks through Diasporic epistemologies affords sensibilities to fecund an understanding of Black life as situated through the psychic terrain of coloniality (Wynter, 2003).

One method of writing Black life as a diachronic approach is to note that particular experiences of Black life result from traversing within and across historical archives of nation-state citizenship. Here, I am thinking about how historical archives become enacted through museums, oceans, flags, text, and national artifacts (Sharpe, 2016) and at the same time shape the sociomaterial terms and conditions that immutably evoke the memory of Black life. Memory then becomes assembled at one level through public documentation that invariably encodes meaning and experiences of Blackness. At another moment we have memory of Black life being lived and archived through oral histories, ancestral knowledge, and cultural enactments. Embodied within this memory are Diasporas with their specific epistemes as constituted through histories of place and time—histories that are resilient to the hegemonic documentation of Black life and have surreptitiously worked to form modes of displacement within particular governing public spheres. This is to also note that concomitant to these histories are sociomaterial practices that come into relations of resistance with the governing coloniality of power, at the same time productive of particular terms and conditions as a way of becoming human for Black life. What I am troubling here when working with the idea of writing history as a social method of inquiry is to acknowledge history is written from different experiences, epistemological assumptions, and philosophical paradigms as culturally shaped through an embodiment of time and place. It is also to say such an inquiry becomes circumscribed with practices imbued through colonial documentation of Black life. Critical writing of Black life ought to vigorously conceptualize these embedded contestations residing within history to tend to the diverging and converging contours that embody Black oral histories, as these subjugated histories are colonially interwoven.

Three distinct moments emerge here, one of which confronts history as a signifier of Blackness resulting materially in disenfranchisement, debasement, and devalued forms of representation of Black life. The second speaks to the disjunctures governing the innumerable historical beliefs, customs, values, and culture of Black life as these moments congeal through shared histories of the Middle Passage (Wright, 2015). And thirdly, the epistemological interest that continuously negates knowledge residing in Black geographies. To write Black life cognizant of such trajectories is, to some extent, to disrupt colonial histories of knowledge by way of opening possibilities for Black life through a language that unremittingly probes what was said, the unsaid, and what needs to be said about Black life. One can imagine in trying to ascertain such practices of Black life is to unearth congruent experiences of coloniality with predispositions to essentialism and absolute debasing conceptions of identity. By contradistinction, Black life can be typified through Middle Passage memory to cogitate about situatedness, place, and future economic pathways as organized by current arrays of social settings within said public spheres of the nation-state. Such writings of Black life make anew ethical promulgations that could respectfully account for the racial disjuncture embedded within history, and work toward embracing alterity that avows the future through an immediate present. In this way attending to Black life can fecund meaning-making sensibilities that differ from archived essentialist texts.

Given the periodization of history in the context of African enslavement, the emphasis is on the past and present alike. In that, understanding the relationship between coloniality and Blackness entails making sense of the formation of Black history with respect to time and place, one that vehemently tends to sociocultural and economic growth, institutional and structural barriers, and quality of life (Dei, 2017). This involves working with an arrangement of alterity that becomes traversed by way of compound Diasporic temporalities, acting intermittingly through diverging and converging paths, resulting not necessarily in some totalizing negation of history, but one that works to create ecological continuities with particular linkages to the land, humanism, social values, and cultural traditions. The pedagogical necessity here is with writing Black life through an intelligible comprehension of Diasporic sensibilities as entrenched in the present. It involves engaging in reading and writing Black life as constituted through transatlantic movement to understand historical interpellations of citizenship, the integration of Black life as localized within imperial Americas, and the particular Diasporic conditions on Black life within the Americas.

Working through this Diasporic epistemic formation affords a method of determining how to broach the many tensions amid theory and practice, to instead allow for the pursuit of a mode of thinking that can attend to histories of Black life as these histories materially become coalesced to some essentialist present. We ought to be cognizant of the layering of problems encoded in such a pursuit. For writing Black life involves a hermeneutic sense as imbued through experience and contextualized diachronically to the phenomenon under inquiry. If we are thinking of Black life through oppression, disenfranchisement, housing, unemployment, and social health, then these instances ought to be thought of from a close reading of particular moments, such as colonization, African enslavement, nation-state, and modernity. To situate Black life within the politics of social economies involves concomitantly addressing the conditions of the Middle Passage and attending plantation politics that continue to provide material readings of experiences of Black peoples. In one instance, the futurity of Black life concerns writing against contingent racial codifications. Whereupon, writing Black life as a social method of inquiry has to be absconded from the circuitous colonial grip that continues to offer formations, contours, and pathways regarding how Black life comes to make sense of the past and how Black life can be realized and accomplished in the present and future. This brings us to some of the ethical concerns regarding the politics of writing Black life. To say this, then, I am less interested in some utopian totality, a writing of Black life that makes permanent a suggestion of avowal, which discursively works to invest within historical linear narratives of progress to distinguish elements of economic growth for Black peoples. In terms of ethical considerations, one ought to be aware of the proximity of being seduced to political representations of being modern that serves the undoing of Black life.

As a method of social inquiry, relocating the politics of black life allows one to interpret the local and the global situatedness of Blackness. Relocation also allows one to interpret the ensuing nation-state itself as being transhistorical and political, providing for the self-determination of Black life beyond the parochial confines of the sovereign nation-state and engendering sociocultural and economic growth within existing post-plantation territories. I can think of two moments arising here, that, for Black life to think of home, to think of Africa, was to think of the present, the here and now, at the same time, home materialized through a dialectical reading of Africa, the Caribbean, and the Americas. If we are thinking of what is at stake politically and intellectually with Black life, then situating transatlantic histories becomes a necessary site of intervention to understand the syncretized experiences of Black life as transnational, cosmopolitan, and constituted through discontinuous histories. Through these discontinuous histories, one of the tasks with writing Black life is seeking to relocate Black life in ways that allow for a cultural undoing of the hegemonic contours of modernity, which inherently de-linked systems of thought that called for ontological linearity to primordial origins (Simmons 2010, 2011).

Making sense of the coloniality immanent within Black life becomes arduous, involving diligent work about speaking to the points of identification and points of dis-identification, points of histories, points of culture, and points of sociality which come to constitute Black social formations. These quotidian points are well augured through memory and oral histories and embedded with sociomaterial forms of the present. Not fixed points that speak to us from the past, as outside of history, waiting to return to through some final, absolute mode of what it means to be human. What does it mean then to be grounded to the past through a particular historical continuity? What does it mean to speak to the present through the intervention of history, through discontinuous histories as entrenched within colonialism, Euromodernity, enslavement, plantation life, Indentureship, and Euro-Enlightenment narratives? And how do we come to understand Black life through these spatiotemporal moments produced through the intervention of history in which Black life is always already produced in and through its continuity? We also need to be cognizant of the cultural inscriptions within the disquiet of Black life. For Black life cannot simply be encapsulated through some binary. Instead, Black life ought to be read through a constitutive historical complexity that through a continuum of ways brings life to a particular place, a particular time that identifies combinatorially with the cultural codifications of the African Diaspora. Writing Black life can invite or facilitate an understanding of belonging, that moves beyond the narrow confines of a boxed belonging to a nation, which speaks to very contained, rigid, performances and desires of knowing the self.

In Closing

Historical terms of citizenship and concomitant ethics have well been spatiotemporally archived as modes of thought and made intelligible through particular sociomaterial practices. Yet Black life and the relationship with the land are asking us to rethink these said modes of thought as accepted "Truth" systems. Black resistance provides for a counter-hegemonic culture that in a sense turns liberal sensibilities of individualism into ethical questions concerning hope, community, and belief in the self as constitutive of different forms of citizenry. For Black life to conceptualize and simultaneously perform a particular type of citizenry as overdetermined against archived ritual practices of late modernity, has in a sense produced a precarious relationship to the historical classificatory system of belonging. The precariousness of Black life remains constantly in question and surreptitiously marked as fugitive within the nation-state. Belonging for Black life invites us to think of how prevailing governmental conditions of the nation-state have interwoven in a profound way encumbered moments and possibilities of the freedoms of citizenry. Shaping a future for Black life might involve asking, what types of citizenship are made possible and through what political philosophies are these futures of citizenry being materially constructed? Indeed, within our present epoch, imagining a social contract that refashions the fugitiveness of Black life into the humanness of citizenry invites addressing the liminal spaces of the entrapments of Black life through such questions of surveillance, risk, security interests, and modes of violence.

First published—Simmons, M. (2019). In G. J. S. Dei, A.V . Jimenez, & E. Odozor. (Eds.), *Cartographies of Blackness and Black Indigeneities* (pp. 51–62). Gorham, ME: Myers Education Press.

References

Browne, S. (2015). *Dark matters: On the surveillance of blackness.* Durham: Duke University Press.
Dei, G. J. S. (2017). *Reframing blackness and black solidarities through anti-colonial and decolonial prisms.* Gewerbestrasse: Springer.
Fanon, F. (1963). *The wretched of the earth.* New York: Grove Press.
Hall, S. (2007). Fundamentalism, diaspora and hybridity. In S. Hall, D. Held, D Hubert, & K. Thompson (Eds.), *Modernity: An introduction to modern societies* (pp. 629–632). Oxford: Blackwell Publishing.
Mbembe, A. (2017). *Critique of black reason.* Durham: Duke University Press.

McKittrick, K. (2006). *Demonic grounds: Black women and the cartographies of struggle*. Minneapolis: University of Minnesota Press.

Mignolo, W. D. (2015). Sylvia Wynter: What does it mean to be human? In K. McKittrick (Ed.), *Sylvia Wynter: On being human as praxis* (pp. 106–123). Durham: Duke University Press.

Sharpe, C. (2016). *In the wake: On blackness and being*. Durham: Duke University Press.

Simmons, M. (2011). The race to modernity: Understanding culture through the Diasporic-self. In N. Wane, A. Kempf, & M. Simmons (Eds.), *The politics of cultural knowledge* (pp. 37–50). Rotterdam: Sense.

Simmons, M. (2010). Concerning modernity, the Caribbean Diaspora and embodied alienation: Dialoguing with Fanon to approach an anti-colonial politic. In G. J. S. Dei & M. Simmons (Eds.), *Fanon and education: Thinking through pedagogical possibilities* (pp. 171–189). New York: Peter Lang.

Simmons, M., & Dei, G. J. S. (2012). Reframing anticolonial theory for the diasporic context. *Postcolonial directions in education*, 1(1), 67–99.

Walcott, R. (2003). *Black like who? Writing black Canada*. Toronto: Insomniac Press.

Wright, M. (2015). *Physics of blackness: Beyond the middle passage epistemology*. Minneapolis: University of Minnesota Press.

Wynter, S. (2003). Unsettling the coloniality of being/power/truth/freedom: Towards the human, after man, its overrepresentation—an argument. *The New Centennial Review*, 3 (3), 257–337.

2.

Locating Black Life within Colonial Modernity: Decolonial Notes

For some time now, the decolonial question has been on the pens of certain scholars (Cabral, 2016; Cesaire, 1972; Fanon, 1963; Nkrumah, 1970; wa Thiong'o, 1986). Within these sensibilities, Blackness endured a precarious relationship with modernity, one lived and made durable through particular sociomaterial enactments, well calcified by way of colonization. Drawing from this relationship, I am curious about how a sociomaterial history of Blackness might contribute to understanding the contemporaneity of Black life, sovereignty, land, and the role of language regarding place. My purpose in writing is to sift through the flotsam of modernity, to understand how emergent relationships within Black life come to make possible sociomaterialized theoretical enactments through the everyday tensions that have typified these relationships. Put another way, I am interested in the circumstances through which Black life comes together, and remains whole, although sometimes fragile under historical pressures, to produce public forces constitutive of knowledge, subjectivities, and multiple modes of identification that come to be organized through a digitized politics of relations in material forms. I am curious about the doing of Black life; how acts of love come to be formed (Freire, 1970); how connections with place come to be; and what social networks are formed, dissolved, or made sustainable. How might we come to know forms of Black life as outside the circumscription of Western exceptionalism? At the same time, what do these relationships mean for decolonial enactments?

My aim is to understand how to come into conscientization (Freire, 1970, 1985) for the decolonized future, one that tends to the intertextual historical encounters of colonial modernity; an encounter that encumbers the African Indigeneity of the Diaspora. My concern here is with making sense of the relational experiences of decolonial life, as these experiences have been cryptically shaped and embodied through histories of memory embedded within the African Diaspora and plantation geographies of enslavement. With this sentiment, my pedagogic hope (Freire, 2011) imbues particular writing cognizant of what places are made possible through colonial modernity, as they come to be racially underpinned through the sociomateriality and epistemic disjunctures of the African Diaspora, simultaneously culminating in a peopling that disrupts the Manichean confines of what it means to be human. Writing through these epistemological curiosities (Freire, 2005), I share some notes I see as necessary for decolonial sense-making.

Ways of Knowing the Decolonial Question

As a starting point, one might begin to imagine how *decolonial* as an interpretive framework can offer different people a place to make sense of their historical and daily experiences. Imagining how decolonization as a practice, as a way of being, as a way of becoming human helps us to understand present-day experiences of Black life through its civil and cultural enactments can be a complex undertaking. How might decolonization help with reading, tracing, and comprehending coloniality within the concomitant conditions of globalization in ways that we can undo dominant forms of performing citizenship? At the same time, if we are thinking about decolonization as a way of knowing our relational experiences, we ought to be cognizant of how particular forms of knowledge come to be made intelligible within Western educational institutions. How and what fields of knowledge are endowed with privilege and installed with discursive authority? In what ways do we become privileged and simultaneously complicit through these disciplinary educational institutions within the current epoch of globalization? How do we become interspersed within educational institutions of late modernity and simultaneously benefit materially from these vantage points?

Given these corollaries, one of the concerns here is with writing *from, with, through, out,* and *against* the academy, that is to say, the tensions of having to write back or be located through some academic or interpretive position and the tensions with experiencing the disciplinary force of having to belong to a particular intellectual genre or tradition. Beyond these tensions are the disciplinary edicts in which the educator becomes accorded and installed through the hallways of institutions with intellectual precedence. Yet these intellectual genres or traditions from which we eloquently write are neither ahistorical, apolitical, neutral, or innocent. Rather, they come with their own ethical concerns, entangled and bound with discursive currency, represented and positioned through the corridors of educational institutions, as well as the public, with discursive capital. As educators, working ethically to undo these entanglements could be an impossibility. It becomes a meaningful learning task when educators implicate the self by thinking about the ways in which we benefit through this epistemic privileging.

I have long spent time working through some of the epistemological questions immanent within decolonial thought to get a sense of the ethics, politics, and implications of doing this work. In particular, and with coming to write this piece, I had to work through the what and how of the ways in which I enter into decolonization. What sort of mindset and orientation of thought are organizing my decolonization process? In doing so, I think about where and how knowledge resides. What are the ways in which knowledge becomes taxonomized through dissimilar geographic locations? What can we know from differently placed spatiotemporal locations regarding the human, community, and ecological spheres? In thinking through these seemingly mundane questions, I trouble the self, my location as a reservoir for knowing, with the focus on what it means to conceptualize decoloniality through self as method. Yet in coming to name these moments, I recognize the flux, temporality, uncertainty, and incommensurability of coming to know; at the same time, I also recognize the pedagogical necessity of making sense of the controversies, contradictions, intersections, and imbrications of these historical conversations.

To think about *decolonial* as a way of doing citizenship involves probing historical forms of knowledge systems and unearthing the masked nexus with such conjunctures of religion, race, gender, sexuality, and able-bodied, linguistic, and techno-bio-diverse ways of belonging to our planet, as well as the concomitant production of modes of inclusion and exclusion within particular public spheres. It involves making sense of how these constructs of knowledge—through intergenerational memory constituted through land, time, and space relations—and embodiment of knowledge become documented, recovered, and put into practice differently by citizens through variant methods and dynamic processes of immersing and engaging the self with digital technology.

Of interest is the making sense of dominant productions of knowledge, as governed through institutional forms of education, and reimagining public spaces for teaching and learning (Kincheloe, 2010). The aim is not necessarily with dismantling educational institutions in the immediate, but rather with undoing systems of knowing about the ways in which dominant knowledge becomes constituted; how particular ways of teaching and learning come to be experienced as the imposition of a determining set of values. I should also mention, with this discussion I am less interested in furnishing or operating calmly in an epistemological system that has historically negated particular peoples from being human and simultaneously expositing certain peoples as being the *preferred* human. I am more concerned with finding possibilities for understanding different ways of being detached from the tacit practices of complying and rewriting the hegemonic canon of knowledge as installed by Western systems. Instead, might we think of decolonization as a creative force, a creative set of processes that reconsiders rewriting the dominant worldview that has come to govern how we experience what it means to be human, what it means to be a citizen as organized by the nation-state in late modernity (Abdi, 2013; Dei, 2017;

Escobar, 2007; Grosfoguel, 2007; Maldonado-Torres, 2007; Mignolo, 2014; Quijano, 2007).

In probing the swarm of disciplinary discursive strategies embedded within the trope of citizenship we might turn to digital technologies (Browne, 2015)—to consider how digital technologies could help with reimaging the disciplinary terms and conditions of knowing and performing citizenship as installed through the many channels of educational institutions (Freire, 2001, 2005). In that, the nation-state citizen becomes a product of discourses that over time has fossilized and made to appear as some natural way of being human. Perhaps by unmasking the variegated performativity of citizenship, we can bring to the surface some of the dominant preconditions through which what it means to be human are made possible. Such knowledge is necessary for coming into the different practices of decolonization. Yet in order for citizenship to be made valid by the nation-state, it is always already purposed within a discursive code of conduct. The concern here with decolonization is with knowing how and what sensibilities are made possible when particular technological attachments become cultural signifiers encoded within everyday practices to shape and situate citizenship in the public sphere (Browne, 2015). What aspects of disciplinary forms of power become uncovered through the differential operations of technology?

I am suggesting that decolonial ways of knowing allow for an underwriting that interprets how sensibilities of being human come to avow and congruently disavow negotiations within colonial-modernity, through embodied polities of the archetype abject-human, that of blackness. Decolonial ways of knowing involve forms of thinking of the world which are relational, constitutive, and dialectically contoured through place, peoples, and incommensurability of becoming (Freire & Macedo, 2001; Freire, 2005). It encompasses historical engagements with Euro-Enlightenment knowledge constructs that come to situate the sociomaterial terms and conditions of the human within the continuous hegemonic production of colonial modernity. Decolonial ways of knowing involve working through difference; they involve coming to write and dialogue through acts of love, with the pedagogic hope of transformative possibilities to undo hegemonic sociomaterial, incommensurable structures and procedures within colonial public spheres (Freire, 1970, 2001, 2011).

In a sense, decolonization concerns understanding how power, questions of belonging, Euro-Enlightenment-knowledge epistemes, and sensibilities of being human come to be enacted and simultaneously circumscribed through the spatial procedures of colonial modernity (Mignolo, 2015). If as a placeholder we were to draw from the sensibility that knowledge becomes socially created through ensuing relationships of practice, as well as what Wynter and Scott (2000) call for—a re-historicization through ethnohistories—then such knowledge becomes provisional for different social imaginaries of being human. What then are the underpinning values and assumptions with one's situated knowledge, and how do these politically laden enactments become embedded within and inform decolonial approaches? We also need to be cognizant of how such situated knowledge as experienced through historical forms of oppression becomes placed within institutions, simultaneously forming scaffolded relations with ongoing educational typologies (Freire, 1970).

Black Life, Knowledge, and the Text

Throughout history, the textbook has played a particular role in determining the qualitative conditions regarding Black life. Textbooks have been installed institutionally within educational settings, as well as public settings such as libraries and museums, in ways that congeal the past and present to shape narratives of Black life. How is Black life enacted, lived, and made to be remembered through the temporalities of the textbook? What are the ways in which Black life remembers or comes to know the self through the assemblage of Atlantic enslavement as textualized and organized through language, artifacts, and digitized print? How does such a historical assemblage become thought of and tacitly interpreted through Enlightenment narratives? Textbooks give us certain relations with knowing, with remembering Black life, with the becoming of Black life, and how Black life comes to be, giving rise to present questions concerning the role of memory regarding belonging in the context of the nation state (Freire & Macedo, 2001).

In terms of the text, Black life has been written and re-written in ways that have honed the diminution of belonging outside of Middle Passage coloniality (Wright, 2015). Notably, the archived presence of Black belonging as inscribed through cities, museums, public spaces, stamps, and libraries has in some ways methodically been concealed within state-imbued Euro-Enlightenment epistemes of modernity (Ferreira da Silva, 2015; Lowe, 2015). The result here is the representation of Black life through absence and different frames of inferiority, promulgating limiting conditions onto what it means for Black life to be responsible for their very said humanness.

Though colonization set out to portray unbecoming systems of relations regarding what it means to be Black, Black life yielded discernible schemas of sensibilities to think about the colonial forays that bound their determining terms and conditions (Wynter, 2003; Wynter & McKittrick, 2015). These sensibilities congealed to spatially form epistemological Diasporas, and through time became transoceanically sedimented within different Black communities (Wynter, 1995a, 1995b, 1997). Traversing across geographies and augured through decolonial, anticolonial, antiracism, postcolonial, and cultural studies, within undergraduate and graduate programs in educational research and social inquiry, these epistemological Diasporas could provide sensibilities to think about Black life, futurities of Black life, as well as the becoming and unbecoming of Black life. Such sensibilities ought to be interwoven with a politics that speaks to the Black self in relation to the historical present and shared ways of knowing Middle Passage cartographies. Insofar as Black life emerged from Atlantic enslavement through colonial modernity, it comes to be materialized through multiple instantiations with the world. In that, Black life is very much embedded with global overtones, as augured through a sociogenesis (Fanon, 1967; Wynter, 2001) that configures the social and the material relations of the becoming of Black life in which they are entwined. Black life, inchoate to plantation geographies (McKittrick, 2006), was interconnected to Indigeneity, indentured laborers from Asia, and African peoples through colonizer governmentality (Lowe, 2015; Scott, 1995). Enmeshed in these complex histories are material relations of violence as contoured through resistance narratives, social death, memory, grief, dispossession of land, mourning, hauntings, and disenfranchisement—all propertized into ritual enclaves of modernity (Mbembe, 2017). While these enclaves distributed possibilities for becoming through encoded cultural beliefs, Black life imprinted multiplicities of formations to survive colonial apparatuses of civility, citizenship, sovereignty, and being human in these emergent geographies.

I am also concerned with what I refer to as the typology of Black life, which I suggest speaks to the spatial, temporal, and relational interactions as they come to materialize through difference, race, historical memory, place, peoples, and communities, and made durable through a multiplicity of sensibilities (McDermott & Simmons, 2013). At the same time, one must remain mindful of ethical considerations: There exists a particular proclivity to reduce Black life to a singular homogenous read that essentializes belonging to sameness. I am more concerned with the folding and unfolding of Black life in response to existing colonial entanglements as enabled through their situated environments, be it secured, unstable, or volatile. Underpinning my thinking is the sensibility of conceptually tracing the *what, how,* and *where* of Black life; its relatedness; and synchronized enactments. This triad presents the complexity of having to unravel how this ongoing relatedness within Black life becomes performed and made durable through particular conditions. Relatedness can also open decolonial approaches to the untold interconnected practices of Black life. It allows for a reading of Black realities to understand social, political, and economic enablement as governed through congeries of indeterminacy, one that notes the distributive effects, sites of attachment, modes of interest, and points of passage, where the becoming of Black life is enacted.

As the realities of Black life come to be reshaped through a host of experiences, belonging for Black life as situated through different forms of ontology, variably becomes re-contoured and re-bound, materializing in a sense through different relations distributed through its own politics, its own articulations (Brand, 2001). How then do these politics and articulations, which embody *reservoirs of Black life* (Mbembe, 2017), become embedded within institutional texts and made durable in contemporary educational settings? How might we imagine what it means to teach and learn through these sensibilities as they become enacted within contemporary classrooms? What I am suggesting is that the Middle Passage, as immanent to the African Diaspora, has provided particular sources for Black life, wherein ways of knowing, belonging, cultural enactments, and social growth have come to materialize without some formal articulation or recall of these historic specific sources (Wright, 2015). What emerged though, through different spatial and temporal periodizations of history (Nimako & Willemsen, 2011; Wright, 2015), were theories as peopled through resistance movements regarding Black life, with specific instances to certain geographies, with distinctive characteristics to the territory of the colonial Middle Passage. These resistance movements enmesh the epistemological conduits of theoretical sensibilities embedded within decolonial approaches.

Black life drew upon decolonial sensibilities which yielded a peopling, spirituality, modes of thinking, acculturation, and socialities, all curated through communities as vested to ancestral geographies and survival of Middle Passage journeys (Wright, 2015). These communities have found new positionalities within the contemporaneous spheres of existing Euromodernity. Through these positionalities, memories of the Middle Passage became inscribed within Black Life, producing histories and resulting in sociomaterial enactments such as images, performances, oral narratives, language, and variant cultural expressions (Iton, 2008; Sharpe, 2016; Wright, 2015; Wynter, 1992). My interest here is in making salient the relationships with Black life and these sociomaterial enactments, and how such relations come to organize the needs of Black peoples in particular instantiations inclusive of possibilities and perils (Simmons, 2010, 2011). What are the experiences of Black life in the present nation-state context, as these experiences draw from the knowledge of what it means to be Black through histories of disenfranchisement? What I am suggesting is that Black life always already experiences their worlds through the interstices of the past as traced through events that become implicitly experienced within their governing public spheres. Thus, Black life becomes determined and conditioned through different sets of relations allowing for interconnectivities to the present.

We might think through the obligatory points of the Middle Passage to get a sense of the determining conditions of how Black life comes to understand the self in its contemporaneity—that is, to think of the Middle Passage as being preserved and made durable in the present in ways that actualize Black life. You might say the Middle Passage has all but left us suddenly and quietly, but if we were to think of the historical present of Black life, we begin to notice the folding of regions with vestiges of the Middle Passage (Wright, 2015). For Black life to make claim to these incommensurable practices, as such, involves wittingly or unwittingly being endowed with cultural attachments yielded through Diaspora and modernity alike, with simultaneous recognition of its abject subjectivity within canonized historiographies.

Since the colonization of time, the ubiquity of Black life has been concerning. Emerging from this ubiquity were theoretical constructs, which responded to the sociomaterial worlds of Black life. For when cultures emerging from the Middle Passage come to recognize forays of subjugation in its continuity, they are then forced to look within themselves, their histories, different ways of being, and modes of resistance and survival, to form inextricable nodes of knowledge and practices that can be situated as theory. Such knowledge and practices specific to particular cultures, time periods, geographies, and generations, like the decolonial and anticolonial struggles of the Civil Rights movement and the Haitian Revolution (James, 1993), give us variant ways to understand the situated experiences of Black life and offer possibilities for change that can translate into some material good.

For Black lives to compartmentalize or fragment their social realities from historical situatedness might not culminate into some clean extrication from the cryptic assemblages of Atlantic enslavement and Middle Passage determinants. In the everyday context, Black life endures historically colonial texts and digitized images that have formed edicts onto how they come to be and know their existing places within private and social settings, as well as public and institutional contexts (Browne, 2015). The upshot is often experienced, I think, through intergenerational modes of communication, as these modes become mediated through tensions of synchronic and diachronic forms of dialogue. In that, given the location of the African Diaspora, Black life comes to know the present as distinct from historical connections, while Black life through other Diasporic loci comes to know the self through particular characteristics of a historical present.

Such are the complex entangled constructs of incommensurability concerning the being of Black life. But yet, the claim to some existence as distinct, disjoint, separate from colonial histories that posit abject modes of being on to Black life is in and of itself constituted through enactments of remembering relational experiences as immanent to the African Diaspora. A possible outcome for Black peoples, then, is to rewrite their situatedness within particular public spheres to ontologize in some way their modes of being within their existing sociomaterial realities. In a sense, these enactments encompass oral narratives as sedimented within the African Diaspora through language, culture, place, and difference. Faced with these enactments, Black life, well augured within its heterogeneity, undertook a series of transfigurations as accorded through Diasporic conduits of the Middle Passage.

Decolonial Thinking as a Field of Knowledge

Perhaps we ought to think about how decolonial thought as a field of knowledge has been installed within particular institutions and concomitantly endowed with limiting epistemological plausibility. To be cognizant about how we make intelligible the vagaries whereby decolonial thought comes to be necessitated in our contemporary epoch or the sociomaterial configurations within educational settings. I think collectively in a reflexive manner; some of the necessary decolonial work is with making salient the collaborative roles of educators, social justice activists, subaltern peoples, and the *wretched of the earth* (Fanon, 1963), in constructing decolonial sensibilities. I am also troubling the politics of knowledge, its location, and myriad signals, as well as the varied processes involved in how particular forms of knowledge become embodied and positioned as legitimate and simultaneously institutionalized as "Truth" systems. To me this dialogue also allows for a conscientization of our different subjectivities and relational experiences (Freire, 1970, 1985, 2001, 2005). It allows us to come into decolonial dispositions. In doing so, we can reflexively situate our thoughts in existing public sphere environments, to delineate historical and contemporary gaps with theory and practice concerning decolonial thought, being mindful that coloniality has a particular interest in a thinking that conjures oppression as static, fixed in time, linear, measurable, discontinuous, and remedied through particular state apparatuses inclusive of public sphere conversations, laws, and ad hoc committees. Often coloniality has been reduced to something mythic, as operating in the past, resulting in synchronic markers installed within current conversations about historical oppression. What we have here is a periodization of history that comes to make sense of itself through the governing instantiation of experiences, one which operates by way of discursively re-signifying its terms and conditions to safeguard its own transmission; it is a sociomaterial performative, discursively imbued to typify a practice of knowing which epistemologically guarantees its being.

What decolonial approaches give us are ways of knowing the complex and interwoven textualities in which they were fashioned and emerged, with the diachronic capacity of making sense of the sociomaterial spheres that they relentlessly strive to intercede. One of the challenges for those of us willing to engage in decolonial work is to recognize the embodied histories immanent within the different decolonial locations, and how such histories come to be determined and represented in the present. At the same time, we also need to recognize how decolonial thinking as a field of knowledge comes to be installed and given particular currency in educational institutions, with the epistemological concern being, what counts as knowledge? We ought to be cautious, and think of decolonial sensibilities as socially, historically, culturally, and politically situated, embodied and undertaken through a peopling within a particular context for a particular purpose. Such sensibilities demand dignity, respect, and love, which can yield knowledge credence within the canonized project of thought (Freire, 1970). Decolonial thinking has also troubled the politics of knowledge, institutionalized locations of knowledge, its signification practices, as well the varied processes involved in how particular ways of knowing become embodied, endowed, and positioned as singular hegemonic conduits of knowing.

Our ways of coming to know have been historically apportioned, compartmentalized, and accessed through textual disjunctures of positivism, post-positivism, and certain theories. Within variant academic communities, and in particular decolonial communities, different forms of epistemic resistance have met these spatio-temporal moments of alternative discursive traditions bringing us, I think, to the place of evidence of knowledge as a particular site of contestation within educational research (Denzin, 2011; Kincheloe, 2010). My thinking on this historical debate on evidence is, in a sense, evidence that speaks to questions of measurability, repeated-verified tests, and strategies resulting in a sum relational, rational objective fact that simultaneously purports reliability and validity, which work to organize and inscribe particular institutions and policymakers. Regarding decolonial sensibilities, how then do we posit measurability and repeated-verified tests or strategies onto data that is not readily accessible or retrievable? How do we posit measurability and verified ways of knowing onto the incommensurability of memory? Hence, in the everyday moment, doing decolonial work involves disentangling from the governing colonial complexity, to instead build creative places in which fruitful dialogue might emerge, giving rise to different acts of love (Freire, 1970).

We also need to be cautious when taking into consideration how the interests of the market can unwittingly produce and reproduce the terms and conditions of oppressive educational thought within institutional settings. Institutionalized education that has to meet the interests of markets often results in competition and scaffolding relations of power regarding epistemological content. As Freire (2005) and Freire and Macedo (2001) invite, how might we then take up a social imaginary as imbued through conscientization, which draws on historical narratives to open alternative possibilities that allow one to make sense of cryptic colonial discourses present within the text, classrooms, institutions, and contemporary public spheres?

Let us take the example of language and the construction of Canada as a nation-state to make sense of how colonial contours of language come to legitimize enactments of belonging and citizenry, and the ways in which language comes to distribute modes of currency, simultaneously installing social capital for particular peoples—to think about civic participation and which language becomes delegitimized and what particular cultures, peoples, and relational ways of knowing become excluded. I think we also have to be concerned with contemporary questions concerning civic participation, public and private engagements, and what or how decision-making factors come into being regarding decolonial thought, education, and teaching and learning practices as governed within classroom settings. I am suggesting that in taking up a pedagogy of hope (Freire, 2011), decolonial approaches can be a place for social action and educational change.

Black Life and Landscapes of Relations

Often enough, Black life remains embodied through certain polities of relations (Glissant, 2010) in which Black peoples themselves come to participate or take up particular performatives or desires materializing into this hegemonic corporeal of sport, dance, music, fashion, apparel, technology, institutional knowledge, and fixed roles in the media (Iton, 2008; Weheliye, 2002). Inasmuch, these mediating materials come to participate within Black life in generative ways, reflective of the community, social stratification, scaffold relations, socialization practices, and oppression and power. Thinking of Black life in this sense allows for a reading that can help with tracing how Black life becomes materially entangled and encumbered through nodal points having diverging and converging forms of variance. My point is that these performatives or desires, as taxonomized through the interests of the market, work to form a cognitive registry, wherein Black life becomes, or is made to be, productive through race-based edicts of plantation geographies, which govern the corporeality of Blackness.

One might say that to couple Black life through a material positionality unwittingly brings disembodied meanings. What I am trying to do, though, is to bring a type of relational thinking, to say that Black life becomes constituted and is made contingent in complex socialites, wherein which particular artifacts and certain materials come to act as signifiers or meaning-making processes embedded with its own politics, ontologies, and epistemological upbringing. Decolonial thought threads through these sensibilities to make sense of the conditioning of Black life in terms of people and the material as they appear in the quotidian context. The hermeneutic challenge here is with marking and identifying these everyday interactions that are historically signified through colonial vestiges, and how such coloniality come to fashion Black life. Another challenge for the writing of decolonial sense-making is with noting the knowledge production schemata and how such schemata become installed within institutional settings. I want to insist that decolonial sensibilities embody the human through a series of knowledge, ethics, values, and cultural beliefs that link onto constellations of material signifiers circumscribing the human within their governing public sphere.

To say survival and resistance were integral experiences to people who have been enslaved or oppressed is an understatement, to say the least. Having said that, part and parcel of decolonial thinking is with denoting how the situated processes of resistance, ensuing socializing formations, and organizing principles become generative of ways of knowing (Cabral, 2016), which simultaneously become inscribed into heuristic perspectives counterhegemonic to colonial narratives which flood everyday Black life. We ought to be mindful of how this deluge flows through institutions, public memory, and a multiplicity of texts to set in place an arrangement of thought that works to ontologically negate Black life. At the heart of the matter here is the question of power, more so the hidden circuitous performative of power (Foucault, 1980), how narratives come to be written, and what stories of Black life are told through such a performative. How does power come into play when Blackness negotiates their place within cities, institutions, and local communities, and the manner in which the terms and conditions of these negotiations come to materialize in particular enactments of demeanor, movement, authorship, and the problematization of everyday concerns of Black life as underpinned through racial classificatory systems. This brings me to the crux of my concerns with Black life and the necessity for decolonization in the context of colonial modernity. Here, I am worried about how Black people assemble and make wholesome the chunks and remnants of the Diaspora which constitute their becoming; how at times within their relational experiences they tacitly mark moments as being codified through race, to in turn have this said racial codification transform into a typification that opens a fluid heterogeneous assemblage with linkage to power and self-determination (Davies, 2008; Foster, 2007; Gilroy, 1993; Hall, 2007; Small, 2018; Stephens, 2005; Walcott, 2014).

I imagine some sensibilities of decolonial thought are always already empirically grounded within the corporeality of resistance—sensibilities that are contextual, distributive, interwoven with imbrications, relational, incomplete, and contestable. So, consolidation of decolonial thinking as reduced to a singular sealed panacea is less the interest here. Rather, decolonial thinking is unswerving with its politics; it demands social justice and institutionalized enablement of its epistemological recognition involving dissimilar modes of probing. I would be remiss not to say that as emerging through geographically specific social movements, decolonial thinking encompasses a scope of ways of knowing, practices, processes, communicative exchanges, materials, and technologies that traverse through multiple loci. I should also follow up with the idea that this scope is produced by way of events, cultural difference, becoming, resistance, and through a particular set of relations that are made cohesive across variant encumbering, contradictions, and indeterminacy. This, though, is the potential of decolonial thought, the capacity to attend to contingent collations as sequenced through ontological difference, while insisting on civic responsiveness to the experiences immanent to Black life. Decolonial thought is more so concerned with the composition of context and power, emergent relational experiences, and the provisionality of resistance that continuously works through the material orderings constituted by difference and epistemological disjunctures.

Black life has an abundance of ontologies, ensconced with colonial entanglements, situated ethics, and political desires historically interwoven through past, present, and future. These spatiotemporal junctures hint at the capacity of Black life to synthesize with continuity—Diasporic memory as contemporaneously lived. Being interpellated through multiple heritages puts Blackness in a dialogue with its compound life forms, at local and global moments. Here we have diverging and converging social interactions enmeshed through intergenerational memory of Black life. From Black forms of life being governed through histories of disenfranchisement, abject subjectivities, and political alienation, we can be attuned to such a traversal, to note how Blackness and the ensuing assemblage of relations come to identify with a sense of self, and make new life forms amid the debasing narratives neatly tucked away within the historiographies of colonial modernity.

Sociocultural and political alienation of Blackness have this way of presenting themselves in a manner where negation of Black life becomes quotidian, putting in place an attitude, a way of being, one of compliance to hegemonic narratives, that divests from the Black self. To help in dispensing with these narratives, I suggest the following questions: How are nation-state formations of belonging being rendered, and what are the ongoing assumptions, attributes, and qualities being engendered in collective or individualized arrays specific to particular cultural histories? What forms of belonging continue to be imagined through particular cultural articulations and gestures? Given the contextual histories, what regulatory, discursive, and material mechanisms were actively deployed to distribute such alienating articulations of Blackness?

There is an implicit way in which the hue of the corporeal is conceptualized, made certain, accepted, and becomes an instrument of understanding Black life. Yet hue, as a cognitive instrument, brings forth a materiality that constitutes a mode of subjectification, whereby Black corporeality simultaneously expresses and transmits forms of governmentality onto the self, giving rise to decolonial knowledge where Blackness, as a cognitive tool, circumvents the limitations and conditions of possibility for meaning-making. What I am suggesting here is that there exists an ontological alterity, historically conditioned through Black life, which, when strategically deployed as a technology of self (Foucault, 1997), can materialize the becoming of Blackness, as well as promote the fashioning of decolonial notes. This also brings us to one of the challenges of decolonial work, that is, having the capacity to form community through certain arrays of leadership, which invites thinking differently about self-determination in the context of sovereignty. I am imagining such decolonial work involves courage concomitant with an ethical and political logic that offers alternative ways of understanding what it means to be human as governed (Mignolo, 2014, 2015) within Black life.

Inevitably for Black life, decolonization concerns itself with being human, or should I say working to free the human of the fixed colonial readings producing Blackness. In that, enactments of being human are already codifed through Eurocentric edicts of modernity (Wynter, 2003). Such a reading has been well critiqued by numerous scholars from postcolonial theory, anticolonial frameworks, Black feminist theory, cultural studies, Black studies, queer studies, and decolonial thought (Brand 1998; Hall 2005; Philip 2017; Wynter 1995b). These fields of thought have done well to broach the temporal estrangement that coloniality offers when reading contemporary political landscapes. Prompting discontinuous histories, this temporal estrangement has put into place myriad generational shifts in terms of viewpoints regarding colonization. With recasting Black Life through place, space, and time; through technological embodiment; and through difference, decolonial sensitivities invite formations of belonging that make sense of being through the interwoven-ness of power, resilience, and knowledge production. It offers possibilities for different peoples to reimagine and redesign their futures through dialogue and different acts of love (Freire, 1970).

First published—Simmons, M. (2020) In S.R. Steinberg, & B. Down (Eds.), *The Sage Handbook of Critical Pedagogies* (pp. 205–217). Thousand Oaks: Sage Publication.

References

Abdi, A. A. (2013). Decolonizing educational and social development platforms in Africa. *African and Asian Studies, 12*(1–2), 64–82.

Brand, D. (2001). *A map to the door of no return: Notes to belonging.* Toronto: Vintage Canada.

Brand, D. (1998). *Bread out of stone.* Toronto: Vintage.

Browne, S. (2015). *Dark matters: On the surveillance of blackness.* Durham: Duke University Press.

Cabral, A. (2016). *Resistance and decolonization.* Translated by Dan Wood with Introductions by Reiland Rabaka & Dan Wood. London: Rowman & Littlefield International.

Cesaire, A. (1972). *Discourse on colonialism.* New York: Monthly Review Press.

Davies, C. B. (2008). *Left of Karl Marx: The political life of black communist Claudia Jones.* Durham: Duke University Press.

Dei, G. J. S. (2017). *Reframing blackness and black solidarities through anti-colonial and decolonial prisms.* Gewerbestrasse: Springer.

Denzin, N. (2011). The politics of evidence. In N. K. Denzin & Y. S. Lincoln (Eds.), *The Sage handbook of qualitative research* (4th ed., pp. 645–657). Thousand Oaks, CA: Sage Publication.

Escobar, A. (2007). Worlds and knowledges otherwise. *Cultural Studies, 21*(2), 179–210.

Fanon, F. (1967). *Black skin white masks.* New York: Grove Press.

Fanon, F. (1963). *The wretched of the earth.* New York: Grove Press.

Ferreira da Silva, D. (2015). Before man: Sylvia Wynter's rewriting of the modern episteme. In K. McKittrick (Ed.), *Sylvia Wynter: On being human as praxis* (pp. 90–105). Durham: Duke University Press.

Foster, C. (2007). *Blackness and modernity: The colour of humanity and the quest for freedom.* Montreal: McGill-Queen's University Press.

Foucault, M. (1997). Technologies of the self. In P. Rabinow (Ed.), *Michel Foucault: Ethics, subjectivity and truth (The essential works of Michel Foucault, 1954–1984, volume one)* (pp. 223–251). New York: The New Press.

Foucault, M. (1980). *Power/knowledge: Selected interviews and other writings 1972–1977.* New York: Pantheon Books.

Freire, P. (2011). *Pedagogy of hope: Reliving pedagogy of the oppressed.* New York: Continuum.

Freire, P. (2005). *Teachers as cultural workers: Letters to those who dare teach.* Cambridge, MA: Westview.

Freire, P. (2001). *Pedagogy of freedom: Ethics, democracy and civic courage.* New York: Rowman & Littlefield.

Freire, P. (1985). *The politics of education: Culture, power and liberation.* CT: Bergin & Garvey.

Freire, P. (1970). *Pedagogy of the oppressed.* New York: Continuum.

Freire, P., & Macedo, D. (2001). *Literacy: Reading the word and the world.* London: Routledge.

Gilroy, P. (1993). *The Black Atlantic: Modernity and double consciousness.* Cambridge, MA: Harvard University Press.

Giroux, H. (2011). *On critical pedagogy.* New York: Continuum.

Glissant, E. (2010). *Poetics of relations.* Ann Arbor: The University of Michigan Press.

Grosfoguel, R. (2007). The epistemic decolonial turn. *Cultural Studies, 21*(2–3), 211–223.

Hall, S. (2007). The global, the local, and the return of ethnicity. In S. Hall, D. Held, D. Hubert, & K. Thompson (Eds.), *Modernity: An introduction to modern societies* (pp. 623–629). Oxford: Blackwell Publishing.

Hall, S. (2005). New ethnicities. In D. Morley & K. Chen (Eds.), *Stuart Hall: Critical dialogues in cultural studies* (pp. 441–449). New York: Routledge.

Iton, R. (2008). *In search of the black fantastic: Politics and popular culture in the post-civil rights era.* Oxford: Oxford University Press.

James, C. L. R. (1993). *American civilization.* Cambridge, MA: Blackwell Publishers.

Kincheloe, J. L. (2010). *Knowledge and critical pedagogy: An introduction.* Gewerbestrasse: Springer.

Lowe, L. (2015). *The intimacies of four continents.* Durham: Duke University Press.

Maldonado-Torres, N. (2007). "On the coloniality of being: Contributions to the development of a concept." *Cultural Studies, 21*(2–3), 240–270.

Mbembe, A. (2017). *Critique of black reason*. Durham: Duke University Press.

McDermott, M., & Simmons, M. (2013). Embodiment and the spatialization of race. In G. J. S. Dei & M. Lordan (Eds.), *Contemporary issues in the sociology of race and ethnicity: A critical reader* (pp. 153–168). New York: Peter Lang.

McKittrick, K. (2006). *Demonic grounds: Black women and the cartographies of struggle*. Minneapolis: University of Minnesota Press.

Mignolo, W. D. (2015). Sylvia Wynter: What does it mean to be human? In K. McKittrick (Ed.), *Sylvia Wynter: On being human as praxis* (pp. 106–123). Durham: Duke University Press.

Mignolo, W. D. (2014). Further thoughts on (de)coloniality. In S. Broeck & C. Junker (Eds.), *Postcoloniality-decoloniality-black critique: Joints and fissures* (pp. 21–51). New York: Campus Verlag.

Nimako, K., & Willemsen, G. (2011). *The Dutch Atlantic: Slavery, abolition and emancipation*. London: Pluto.

Nkrumah, K. (1970). *Consciencism: Philosophy and ideology for decolonization*. New York: Modern Reader.

Oliver, K. (2004). *The colonization of psychic space*. Minneapolis: University of Minnesota Press.

Philip, M. N. (2017). *Blank: Essays and interviews*. Toronto: Book*hug.

Quijano, A. (2007). Coloniality and modernity/rationality. *Cultural Studies, 21*(2), 168–178.

Scott, D. (1995). Colonial governmentality. *Social Text, 43*, 191–220.

Sharpe, C. (2016). *In the wake: On blackness and being*. Durham: Duke University Press.

Simmons, M. (2011). The race to modernity: Understanding culture through the Diasporic-self. In N. Wane, A Kempf, & M. Simmons (Eds.), *The politics of cultural knowledge* (pp. 37–50). Rotterdam: Sense.

Simmons, M. (2010). Concerning modernity, the Caribbean Diaspora and embodied alienation: Dialoguing with Fanon to approach an anti-colonial politic. In G. J. S. Dei & M. Simmons (Eds.), *Fanon and education: Thinking through pedagogical possibilities* (pp. 171–189). New York: Peter Lang.

Small, S. (2018). Theorizing visibility and vulnerability in Black Europe and the African Diaspora. *Ethnic and Racial Studies, 41*(6), 1182–1197.

Stephens, M. (2005). *Black empire: The masculine global imaginary of Caribbean intellectuals in the United States, 1914–1962*. Durham: Duke University Press.

Walcott, R. (2014). The problem of the human: Black ontologies and the "coloniality of our being". In S. Broeck & C. Junker (Eds.), *Postcoloniality-decoloniality-black critique: Joints and fissures* (pp. 93–105). New York: Campus Verlag.

wa Thiong'o, N. (1986). *Decolonising the mind: The politics of language in African literature*. Oxford: James Currey. Nairobi: EAEP. Portsmouth, NH: Heinemann.

Weheliye, A. G. (2002). Feenin: Posthuman voices in contemporary black popular music. *Social Text 20*(2:71), Summer, 21–47.

Wright, M. (2015). *Physics of blackness: Beyond the middle passage epistemology*. Minneapolis: University of Minnesota Press.

Wynter, S. (2003). Unsettling the coloniality of being/power/truth/freedom: Towards the human, after man, its overrepresentation—an argument. *The New Centennial Review, 3: 3,* 257–337.

Wynter, S. (2001). Towards the sociogenic principle: Fanon, identity, the puzzle of conscious experience, and what it is like to be "black". In M. F. Duran-Cogan & A. Gomez-Moriana (Eds.), *National identities and socio-political changes in Latin America* (pp. 30–66). New York: Routledge.

Wynter, S. (1997). Columbus, the ocean blue, and fables that stir the mind: To reinvent the study of letters. In B. Cowain & J. Humphries (Eds.), *Poetics in the Americas: Race, founding and textuality* (pp. 141–163). Baton Rouge: Louisiana State University.

Wynter, S. (1995a). 1492: A new world view. In V. L. Hyatt & R. Nettleford (Eds.), *Race, discourse, and the origin of the Americas* (pp. 1–57). Washington, DC: Smithsonian Institute.

Wynter, S. (1995b). The pope must have been drunk, the king of castile a madman: Culture as actuality, and the Caribbean rethinking modernity. In A. Rupercht & C. Taiana (Eds.), *The reordering of culture: Latin America, the Caribbean and Canada (in the hood)* (pp. 1–41). Ottawa: Carleton University Press.

Wynter, S. (1992). Rethinking "aesthetics": Notes towards a deciphering practice. In M. Cham, (Ed.), *Ex-iles: Essays on Caribbean Cinema* (pp. 237–279). New Jersey: Africa World Press.

Wynter, S., & Mc Kittrick, K. (2015). Unparalleled catastrophe for our species? Or, to give humanness a different future: Conversations. In K. McKittrick (Ed.), *Sylvia Wynter: On being human as praxis* (pp. 9–89). Durham: Duke University Press.

Wynter, S., & Scott, D. (2000). The re-enchantment of humanism: An interview with Sylvia Wynter. *Small Axe, 8,* 119–207.

3.

Politics of Urban Diasporized Youth and Possibilities for Belonging

The unabated influx of Diasporized youth within the flotsam of colonial empire has given rise to a range of complex experiences regarding youth, Diaspora and the interplay of colonial modernities. Diaspora and youth studies have emerged as disciplines that critically engage these politics. These disciplines also contribute to understanding how different people, spaces, and lived experiences of the "Other" have come to be textually framed through counter-narratives. This discussion seeks to understand the experiences of diverse Urban Diasporized youth that have historically emerged through the Caribbean Diaspora, and who, through struggle and resiliency, have worked to change social conditions that carry the vestiges of colonialism. As part of the larger fields of Diaspora and youth studies, the chapter queries the transatlantic experiences of Urban Diasporized youth who emerged from the Caribbean Diaspora in order to understand the particular cultural practices they engage in to come to know the self and to understand what it means to be human as they negotiate their contemporary political and cultural landscapes. The study of these Urban Diasporized youth provides alternative ways of knowing and understanding how youth come to actualize the self, and what it means to belong to the nation-state that is relevant for youth studies and critical social theory. It offers different ways of interpreting citizenry as experienced in Western culture, which could inform transformative practices for social science research. Understanding this diverse form of knowledge can help educators and policy makers re-conceptualize learning in the context of conventional education in order to promote inclusive schooling. Holistically, the discussion is meant to engender critical discernment concerning youth leadership as contextualized within the everyday Diasporic public sphere life of youth culture.

Learning Objectives and Research Questions

As noted, the chapter seeks to understand the lived experiences of Urban Diasporized youth and how these experiences are shaped by concepts of race, culture, nationalism, and ethnicity. My learning objectives concern the ways in which these youth come to understand race within the public sphere of the Western nation-state and center on the following questions: What are the ways in which Urban Diasporized youth come to understand race and ethnicity through their transatlantic histories? By what means does the understanding of race and ethnicity by Urban Diasporized youth organize and inscribe their political identities? In particular, I am concerned how social desires, cultural discontinuities, and embodied ways of knowing of these diverse Urban Diasporized youth come to be shaped through the Diaspora and simultaneously become organized and configured through the governing cultural terrain of the Western public sphere. From the onset let me say my interest in the Diaspora is less with the etymological construct, nor am I speaking about a totalizing experience of exile, though at moments exile is part and parcel of the Diasporic experience. With Diaspora, I am thinking of process, I am thinking of the movement of people to different geographies, such as transatlantic, transoceanic movement from Britain to Africa to the Caribbean and Euro-Americas, a movement whereby historically people come to know themselves through the margins of their contemporary public sphere. Consequently, I am interested in a sociocultural reading of the different political identity formations of urban youth, particularly, how urban youth come to know and understand the historical discursive racial constellations of the Diaspora. I am concerned with understanding how, in the context of schooling and education, through the Diaspora, the national subject emerges and continues the project of civility as her/his own within the context of the colonial settler nation-state, and how this process aids with entrenching North-South imperial relations. I am more concerned about how urban youth experience citizenry-sovereignty and how this experience forms the conditions of insertion within the nation-state and in what way this sense of insertion comes to govern the integrative potentiality of Diasporized peoples.

Diaspora as Method

I foreground the discussion by writing autoethnography by way of Diaspora as method (Ellis, 2009; Ellis & Bochner, 2000; Pinar, 1994; Reed-Danahay, 1997; Richardson, 2000; Roth, 2005; Wolcott, 2004). Through this method, I intervene by way of Diasporic sensibilities that speak to the colonial specificities that ethnocentrically privilege power within historical educational institutions. I am particularly concerned with how contemporary Diasporized national-subjects come to be regulated. What are the contemporary polities of resistance to Diasporized citizenship? Writing autoethnography through Diaspora as method involves disembedding the complex cultural practices of urban youth that have been historically silenced through the colonial racial schema (Fanon, 1967). In our contemporary epoch, to write Diaspora suggests speaking through particular constellations of imperialism, transnationalism, the nation-state, the national-subject, race, culture, ethnicity, sexuality, religion, migration, refugees, and given the events of 9/11 the emerging classification of terrorist. What we are left with is a series of discontinuities as these discontinuities continue themselves through particular cultural predilections. My interest is in understanding how Urban Diasporic youth make sense of their cultural affiliations as discursively produced through its ontology.

Thinking about Diasporic subjectivities involves understanding how power, knowledge, and privilege come to be enacted and simultaneously circumscribed through the spatial procedures of race. The challenge here is with finding ways Urban Diasporized people come into some sense of agency, in particular how local historic ways of knowing the Diaspora come to engage, come to dialogue with Euromodernity. My interest, too, has been with the everyday conceptualization of desire by urban youth, about the way desire comes to be maneuvered, and concomitantly producing of urban subjectivities, that is, to think about how the variant life choices of Diasporic people come to be contingent or mutually exclusive upon colonial modernity. Needless to say, these moments speak to questions of accessibility, about cultural memories of Indigenous ways of knowing. It speaks to the contradictions of the culturally mediated past and present, to the movement of African peoples in which ontological histories encounter the colonial modalities of modernity, an encounter which coalesces the Indigeneity of the Diaspora, the colonial-civility of Euromodernity into this national-subject, that of the sovereign citizen within settler nation-state (Bauman, 2004; Dei & Simmons, 2012; Foucault, 2007; Giddens, 1991; Habermas, 1998; Kincheloe, 2005, Kincheloe & Steinberg, 2008; Scott, 1995).

I want to locate this encounter as ambivalent to the Diaspora. In that, if we are speaking about race-racism and the ensuing relations of the imperial state and how power-privilege becomes ascribed to the dominant group, Diaspora as method becomes central to discussing these lived moments as they come to be navigated and contoured through race and everyday racism thus calling for a specific theorizing that wills an understanding of what it means to be human as historically circumscribed through the congeries of colonial modernity. It means ethnographically engaging these abject spaces-places, which undoubtedly are rife with uncertainty, transgression, spirituality, pedagogies, and regularities of the human. It involves coming to know, coming to make sense of one's complicity within local performatives of coloniality. Essentially, I am writing to come to situate what spaces-places are made possible for Urban Diasporized youth through these subjectivities of desire as they come to be racially underpinned to the material, expressions, attitudes, and cultural dispositions of the Diaspora, ultimately culminating in an identity that disrupts the Manichean confines of what it means to be human (Fanon, 1967; Hall, 1997, 2000, 2007).

There always already exist historical conditions of affect immanent within the experiences of urban youth. I turn my attention to Fanon (1963), *The Wretched of the Earth*, where he engages questions of national consciousness, and decolonization through particular ineffable conditions of affect, such as alienation and abjection. Fanon suggests that these moments in their coloniality have been uneven, insofar as they have been embodied through a historical perception of time that speaks concomitantly to the past-present. I am suggesting that these moments of national consciousness, abjection, alienation, and decolonization, as constituted through the Diasporic spatiality of urban youth are part and parcel of urban youth modernities (Gilroy, 1993; Walcott, 2003; Wynter, 1995). Yet, capitalism necessitates the continued colonial production of modernity and saturates itself throughout North-South geographies (Giroux, 2009; Hardt & Negri, 2000; Jameson, 2005). I am suggesting, then, that Diasporized-subjects come to avow, and congruently disavow, their location within capitalist-modernity through embodied polities of the archetype abject-urban youth as lived through essentialism-anti-essentialism, authenticity, cultural homogeneity-heterogeneity, and ethnic sameness-difference. At the same time, I am writing less with reducing the Caribbean Diaspora as to always already being fashioned through the permanence of change, I am suggesting that Urban Diasporic culture immanent within the political sites of resistance calls for recognizing the everyday sociality of intertextual histories as they culminate in the lived experiences of modernity. I am evoking critical educational discursive practices imbued through Diasporic sensibilities that have the potential to resist and disrupt hegemonic patterns of knowledge about Diasporic identity, which have historically subverted possibilities for transformative work, including ethical relations and solidarities in local, national, and transnational academic spaces. My aim is, in a sense, to provide a particular conceptualization for schooling and education that, in effect, provides a peopling for the decolonized future of urban youth.

Placing historical trajectories to Diaspora is key to understanding contemporary questions concerning Diasporized youth, in that, local knowledge about the community, settler, immigrant, race, and nation-state ought to be engaged dialectically when talking about youth citizenship and belonging to a particular urban space. Diasporic sensibilities allow for an articulation of youth citizenry that moves the hegemonic discourse of nation-state citizenry beyond that of its binary confines, from dislocation and belonging or home and exile, to invite more of a historical reading that takes into account, enslavement, imperialism, expropriation of Indigenous lands, the extermination of local peoples, genocide, settlement, and migration. In that, there are multiple embodied bio-histories at play within urban spaces. Bio-histories that ought to recognize shared experiences of colonial affect which makes alternative possibilities for urban solidarity. Historically, sovereignty concerned colonial conquest of Indigenous lands. Cartographised through territories and borders, and legitimized through legal constitutions, the acquisition of land through time has continued to a broader economic sphere. At the same time, the historical procedures of sovereignty have refashioned themselves from colonial conquest of Indigenous lands, to a sense of bio-sovereignty in which Urban Diasporized youth engage in particular performative procedures as inculcated through militarized capitalist transnational cultures of modernity and as culminating as this subject of citizenry. Sovereignty of urban youth then becomes dependent on the performative, which surreptitiously forms integrative platforms within the governing system of urban production. It involves understanding the variant ways urban youth, individually and collectively, move through their surroundings by way of primordial knowledge to traverse their modernities of the present. Much of the conversation about urban youth within the media and public sphere concerns the problematic of youth, a problematic that ultimately culminates in the desiring for final solutions. Hence, the pedagogical requisite to trace these primordial knowledge experiences of urban youth to understand how these primordial moments become discursively refashioned to meet the needs of contemporary society. And how this refashioning of the primordial comes to relocate and reimagine alternative ways of reinserting Diasporized youth within the governing capitalist public sphere.

Diasporized Youth and the Race to Modernity

The cry from the capitalist print (see Anderson, 1991) is that long gone are systems of enslavement, legal institutionalizing of apartheid, Civil Rights movements, anti-racism/anti-colonial struggles, and that racism has retracted itself. But historically racism has always already been a transhistorical experience. Historically racism involved relations to the "Other." Historically, racism concerned modes of production, exploitative social relations, capitalism, and global territorialization. In contemporary neo-colonial times, we are presented with different articulations of racism through state policies that work to exclude and position certain customs, values, and cultures that have historical epistemological roots within Eurocentric traditions. The experience of racism then may not be in the sense of acquisition of colonies, but more so through particular modes of production that move Urban Diasporized youth into different spaces of the capitalist public sphere thereby producing and reproducing the unfreedoms of desire in the form of aestheticized commodities waiting to be consumed. Race and capital have been vital invariants to the movement of urban youth within the myriad constellations of Diaspora and remain critical for urban youth to come into a particular form of belonging in a time when power and privilege have been embedded in the commodification of state-culture. Having an invested interest in these polities allows for Diasporized youth to transport their subjectivities into a particular quality of civic life. Yet the race to modernity involves relocating subjectivities within the colonial capillaries of the technological nation-state in which the racialization of space approaches its fecundity through public sphere socio-politico culture that historically has its epistemes augured in Euro-Enlightenment forms of knowledge. Modernity, then, in and of itself becomes dependent on this sovereign Diasporized subject in ways in which Diasporized youth take up the imperial subject position of the national-subject, insofar as the coloniality contingent to urban spaces circumscribes these said Diasporized people. This, in a sense, speaks to the embodiment of transhistoric territorialization, in that, urban youth, as propertized through sovereignty, become the local territory of the nation-state and concomitantly endowed with the governing politics of capitalist socio-cultural modes of production.

Supposedly, we are in the postracial epoch, yet the proteanism of coloniality articulates itself through educational institutions, capitalist media, citizenry, and state governance, thereby tacitly mediating translocal communicative exchanges of Diasporized youth. The resurgence of class debates has centered the post-racial. Urged through the discourse of militarized imperial globalization, mass media conversations do well to place and locate conversations about exploitation, poverty, employment, healthcare, housing, and issues concerning social justice as ontologically spatial to all communities, trumpeting in a sense that within the governing democracy we all face oppression as discontinuous from colonial histories. Hence, the postracial is inserted and, to some extent, contiguous to the postcolonial allowing for the economic disposition to become the determining variant regarding what it means to be human, what it means to be this re-scripted post-modern citizen as constituted through the pluralization of difference and as materializing through fragmented communities. The paradox here, and what I have come to frame as the ambivalence of the Diaspora, is that as urban youth of the Diaspora come to claim their humanism by contesting the systemic forms of discrimination through race, gender, class, religion, ableism, and language as such, they have willingly participated and continue to participate in these hegemonic relations of the West in which Diasporized youth come into power and privilege as they oath themselves into being this sovereign national-subject, where ultimately the transformed Diasporic youth benefits through the active complicity of the coloniality of capitalist-citizenry. Today with the retooling of globalization, we are faced with pointed questions about human rights and the redistribution of material goods, where ultimately, I think the call suggests reparation. There has been an urgent engagement for social justice needs within the nation-states of the West. My concern is while we engage in contesting the location of equity within the Western metropolis, the imperial agendas between North-South countries are left well in place. Presently, part and parcel of being human is about belonging, that is, identifying with a particular nation-state. It is about borders and territories imperially marking and inscribing the human condition through the culture of bounded geographies.

Historically, primordialism has resided within and beyond these imperial contours and continues to resist these scripted material enticements of the coloniality of globalization. As constituted through the primordial (see also Allahar, 1994), Diasporic sensibilities allow for the movement of peoples as governed through the coloniality of globalization to be counter-hegemonic by the same neo-liberal humanitarianism of the Western nation-state. In a sense then, I am arguing that colonial forms of citizenry can come to be underwritten through Diasporic movement. However, by no means is this some naïve utopian claim to citizenry without a sum critical read concerning the interplay with different histories, about the politics of resistance, self-determination, and survival, that for different bodies these desires play out differently. Within the capitalist production of the nation-state, citizenry and sovereignty have come to concern legitimized insertions, through secured militarized borders while at the same time producing Diasporic movement that has come to be discursively contoured through the tropes of immigrant, refugee, illegality, and foreigner. Keeping with the culture of the imperial order, these tropes are essentially racialized, which continue through histories of colonial time to mark the "Other." To invite Diasporic citizenry through particular thinking of a postnational humanism is to then have to work with the colonial historical trajectories of Indigenous expropriation, transatlantic conditioning of African enslavement, and the desires of difference.

Pedagogy of Diaspora and the Search for Youth Citizenship

Diaspora provides the impetus to usurp historical questions of settler nation-state citizenry by centering complicit capitalist flows of movement, be it labor, goods, services, or commodities. Yet, what historical trajectories constitute this settler national-subject and concomitantly invite Diasporic inclination to permanently participate within these Northern constellations of the human condition? Isin and Wood (1999) amplify certain variants of sovereignty, that of, *territoriality, autonomy,* and *legality,* that these variants as underpinned through militarized violence, posit rights, power, and privilege to certain bodies, insofar as the body becomes interpellated into the human condition of citizenship. Where the Diaspora intervenes is through a particular primordial governmentality that is not readily organized and inscribed as the historical settler nation-state subject came to be reified through the said *territoriality, autonomy,* and *legality* of sovereignty. Diasporized youth come into the variegated forms of the human condition as located within the public sphere of the metropole, transformative of a divergent mode of socializing. One is inculcated through the dispositions, expressions, articulations, practices, perceptions, and attitudes (Bourdieu, 1991) of the Enlightened-subject.

Yet, these newly found dispositions, immanent to the West, offer no guarantee for the Enlightenment public sphere, such that to say the urban youth becomes circumscribed and enveloped in ways that stabilize and fecund the colonial desire of the West is by no means finite and totalizing. Diasporic youth carry with them across space and time histories of resistance, histories of colonial encounters, embodied knowledges that anachronistically speak through the lived experience of transatlantic plantation life. Depending on the degree of decolonization different polities emerge that can help dissipate entrenched colonial attitudes. However, while the Enlightenment public sphere struggles to reconfigure itself through these transplanted Diasporic-polities, the imperial lacuna between the West and Southern countries expands itself in ways that furthers dependency on the West, one of which is through increased migration. Migration as capitalistically imbued allows for Diasporized youth to move into the status-quo of power and privilege through education, occupation, and skilled labor. At the same time, education has delimited certain spaces for the "Othered" body that have come to mark the participatory process of youth citizenship. This demarcation speaks very much to a necessary class analysis of the social field, which, more often than not, becomes discursively pinned to debates concerning equality and meritocracy.

My interest, however, concerning youth citizenry as constitutively formed through the Diaspora is about accountability and responsibility;

it is about the quality of civic life as negotiated through difference. It is about questions regarding Indigenous land. It is about understanding how a series of political configurations, a series of nation-state policies come to self-regulate citizenry/sovereignty in particular spaces, and at the same time how these spaces come to be resisted and contested by urban youth of difference. Historically citizenry has been fixed, homogenous, and always already relational to the nation-state. However, with the emergence of Diasporic fields, Diasporic domains in their material presence come to articulate social inquiries, which speak to the broader colonial experience as reified through the inter-/intra-policies of the imperial formations of the nation-state. The social of the public sphere comes to coalesce itself through cultural difference thereby formulating new polities of representation, which variably culminate into a disquiet predicated on the sum historical indissoluble ethnoracial embodied property. Yet, the Diaspora disseminates knowledges in which institutionalized recognition has been a struggle. Coming to belong, or to identify with a particular nation-state, often places Diasporized youth in contradictory relations to which they have claimed sovereign membership. My interest is in finding ways to challenge the way of being/becoming/performing the national-subject as a bounded relationship with the state.

Perhaps, too, we should consider how urban youth come into being the national-subject, to think about the particular socio-cultural variants being resisted and the particular variants being desired and performed within present-day society. But what are the contemporary forms of desire, resistance, and orientations of belonging? In Toronto, in the summer of 2010 during the occasion of the G20 Summit, there were historical forms of resistance in the downtown public sphere of Toronto. Various interest groups, including youth, marched together for a collective call for social-change/social-justice. At the center of the disquiet was bringing critical awareness for the urgent need to de-imperialize concurrent transmissions of globalization. Put another way, to undo neo-colonial forms of inter-/intra-state policies that work to maintain particular geographies in impoverished axes and also problematize the quality of life, the quality of what it means to be human for particular bodies deemed illegal, refugee, terrorist, foreigner, undocumented worker as such. Yet resistance to the G20 Summit was taken up broadly through different political locals, accorded by different people, underpinned through race, class, gender, sexuality, and ability, in which the irreducible question invariably speaks to the relationship with human rights and becoming the subject of the sovereign citizen. I am thinking about these points of engagement, these points of resistance culminating through shared experiences of the Diaspora, in that the Diaspora is a politics of doing, a politics of becoming, a politics of action.

I think it is important to note that the G20 was well steeped in violence. My politics is not with condoning violence, but more so with placing a historical vector on violence to understand how citizenry of youth and the settler nation-state materialized through this index and how violence plays out in the contemporary moment to will youth citizenry into being. How might we read a pedagogy of violence as a political act of resistance that ultimately works to de-interpellate the youth subject into the human? How do we come to understand the legitimized protective forces of the state as constitutive of violence? Moreover, the G20 protests marked spaces of youth resistance that endowed belonging differently, that called attention to the unequal distribution of goods, to the question of rights, justice for all, to articulate a critical sense of citizenship that necessitates resistance. Watching this violence play out on television was quite appalling, for I was watching two competing forms of violence, legitimized violence as installed through the state and as inaugurated through various apparatuses, from uniforms, badges, horses, batons to de-legitimized violence, forms of resistance as imbued through critical memory of histories of anti-colonial/anti-imperial/anti-racist movements. What I was witnessing was in a sense the contestation of privilege, in which the diverging forces form themselves through the interests of human rights, social justice, equality, and some sense of freedom. For me, these performative acts of illegitimized violence speak to histories of transformation, histories of resistance for oppressed peoples. Interestingly enough, however, the dominant mass media articulation in its presumably neutral, objective, omnipresent posture worked quickly to frame the uncertainties and unresolved tensions of the G20 protests. Yet, in many ways, the G20 protest was about the material. My concern, however, is with the location of the material, in which the contestation of the material as imbued locally might not necessarily speak to the *ownership of the means of production*, but more so to the equitable distribution of commodities, goods and services, and contemporary questions about civil rights, which systemically leave imperial transmissions well in place. If the collective responsibility of the protest spoke to the interest of global equity then I am suggesting critical dialogue as engendered through Diasporic sensibilities which can speak to the necessity of de-imperializing North-South relations.

I am proposing that contemporary forms of desire, resistance, and orientations of belonging precipitate the alterity of the Diaspora (Bhatt, 2004; Pinar, 2000), in ways in which the practices of Urban Diasporized youth cultures even when commodified and packaged become primordially endowed through transoceanic embodiment, which inherently convey transhistorical/transatlantic expressive meanings of emancipation/freedom/liberation of oppressed peoples. What I am suggesting here is that these forms of desire, resistance, and orientations of belonging as immanent to the alterity of Diasporized youth are not mutually exclusive, but more so dependent, constitutive on the immutable ethnocentric Euro-Enlightened subject. What I am interested in is the primacy of the "counter-culture of modernity" (Gilroy, 1993), that these said Urban Diasporized youth cultures develop polities of the present where, through socially stratified configurations of place, Diasporized youth come into spaces of privilege which then become a historically performed as their own. So if we are thinking about the spatiality of race and the way in which currency/capital is accorded to the abject-body, or as Cheryl Harris (1995) aptly notes *whiteness as property*, I am thinking about how these embodied privileged spaces of the Diaspora speak to the delimitation of Diasporic communities as they become colonially uncertained through racialized difference. I would imagine that this calls for a discussion concerning the complexities with difference; historic specificities of colonialism; and the production of whiteness as privileged, gendered, and classed within the congeries of globalization and the nation-state. My concern here is with knowing how these disjunctures come to be whitened and simultaneously blackened through Diasporic-alterity (Ladson-Billings, 2000).

I also think it is important to discuss the tropes of emancipation, liberation, and freedom in the context of the Diaspora as these tropes become situated in the West. Too often urban youth becomes framed as the consumer of post-modern capitalism, as ahistorical, depolitical, as turning one's back from the native homeland, as coopting with the imperial gender, as being complicit with contributing to the impoverishment of Southern countries, as all but desiring to be this Enlightened national-subject (Appadurai, 1996; Gilroy, 1993; Jameson, 2005; Scott, 1995). Part and parcel of my writing is in a sense working to reclaim the Diasporic youth from these enclaves, to instead re-frame the discussion differently concerning the transatlantic experience of the Diaspora and what it means to be human, while at the same time working with the politics and ethics of these essentialist notions that come to totalize the experience of the Diaspora. In doing so, I am not dismissing these essentialist claims. I am, however, marking them as some of the possibilities and I am willing to work with them dialectically as they come to configure the social, the lived experiences of Diasporized peoples. I am framing these spaces as distinctive, for I believe these spaces need to be understood through specific histories, that situate the colonial differently as the colonial comes to reside within the West and the imperialized South. I also recognize these colonial histories are interwoven and constitutive. However, I am arguing that the colonial comes to be lived in the West in ways that are arguably distinguishable from how the colonial comes to be located in the South. In this regard, the matter of culture-and-decolonization is of the utmost importance to this discussion, in that culture and decolonization can help articulate a theory concerning the socio-cultural experience of the Diaspora as these synchronistic experiences become embodied within urban youth.

Conclusion

Notably, theory ought to be specific to particular historical conditions as contingent across place, time, and space. Given the geography of Urban Diasporized youth, we must then speak about certain constitutive variants such as transatlantic-blackness, Indentureship, post-independence, race, and culture. However, with the congeries of white settler nation-state differing itself in ways in which the inauguration of this event called Independence ushered a form of governance where the body historically designated as the abject-plantation-subject becomes relocated in the public sphere as citizen, as national subject, as human. I am asking then, and as precipitated through these specific histories of colonialism, what does it mean to have this sense of a collective national consciousness for urban youth as emerging from these colonial designated spaces of enslavement and plantation? Frantz Fanon (1967), in his *The Wretched of the Earth*, essentially broached this question. Fanon spoke about the necessity of having a national consciousness that engaged the histories of colonialism. For urban youth to have some emancipatory sense would entail having the critical consciousness to engage daily in lived colonial modernities. Fanon cautions about the pitfall for such, that the colonial can re-present itself in ways in which the local takes up the subject position of the privileged thus repeating the colonial through different social practices. Hence, belonging, unbelonging, migrancy, and Diasporic conditions become ontologized within a given geographical domain (Ahmad, 2008).

I am suggesting the dominant mode of political orientation within the spatial communes of urban youth as lived, refashioned and performed, congeal and form itself historically through cultural memories of transhistorical peoples, discursive inscriptions of the governing edicts of capitalism, and the myriad neo-colonial procedures of globalization. This concomitantly work to constitute what it means to be human for urban youth, which as incited through the interests of self-determination has become procured through the material conditions of colonialism. Fanon was quite mindful to distinguish between nationalism and national consciousness, that national consciousness becomes conditioned through culture, that for colonized peoples culture ought to be determined through decolonization, decolonization which can come to qualitatively frame local peoples with de-imperializing attitudes. Having said that, my politics concern the manner in which contemporary material sociocultural artifacts of Urban Diasporized youth become an organizing vector through transhistorical understandings of ontological belonging. What I am interested in is the experience of urban youth concerning these contemporary questions of understanding the self through ontological belonging, as they come to be historically shaped through the social conjunctures of the many cultural formations of modernity. I am considering, then, a necessary theory that speaks to this present Diasporic contiguity. I am imagining a theory that dialectically intervenes through Diaspora as method, one that speaks with the complex histories immanent to the lived social world of Urban Diasporized youth.

First published—Simmons, M. (2014). In A. Ibrahim & S. Steinberg (Eds.). *Critical Youth Studies Reader* (pp. 195–204). New York: Peter Lang.

References

Ahmad, A. (2008). *In theory: Classes, nations, literatures.* New York: Verso.

Allahar, A. L. (1994). More than an Oxymoron: Ethnicity and the social construction of primordial attachment. *Canadian Ethnic Studies, 26*(3), 18–33.

Anderson, B. (1991). *Imagined communities: Reflections on the origin and spread of nationalism.* London: Verso.

Appadurai, A. (1996). *Modernity at large: Cultural dimensions of globalization.* Minneapolis: University of Minnesota Press.

Bauman, Z. (2004). *Wasted lives: Modernity and its outcasts.* Cambridge: Polity.

Bhatt, C. (2004). Contemporary geopolitics and 'alterity' research. In M. Bulmer & J. Solomos (Eds.), *Researching race and racism* (pp. 16–36). London: Routledge.

Bourdieu, P. (1991). *Language and symbolic power.* Cambridge, MA: Harvard University Press.

Dei, G. J. S., & Simmons, M. (2012). Writing diasporic indigeneity through critical research and social method. In S. Steinberg & G. Cannella (Eds.), *Critical qualitative research reader* (pp. 296–306). New York: Peter Lang.

Ellis, C. (2009). *Revision: Autoethnographic reflections on life and work.* Walnut Creek, CA: Left Coast Press.

Ellis, C., & Bochner, A. P. (2000). Autoethnography, personal narrative, reflexivity: Researcher as subject. In N. K. Denzin & Y. S. Lincoln (Eds.), *Handbook of qualitative research* (pp. 733–768). Thousand Oaks, CA: Sage.

Fanon, F. (1967). *Black skin white masks.* New York: Grove Press.

Fanon, F. (1963). *The wretched of the earth.* New York: Grove Press.

Foucault, M. (2007). *The politics of truth.* Los Angeles: Semiotext(e).

Giddens, A. (1991). *Modernity and self-identity: Self and society in the late modern age.* California: Stanford University Press.

Gilroy, P. (1993). *The black Atlantic: Modernity and double consciousness*. Cambridge, MA: Harvard University Press.

Giroux, A. H. (2009). Dirty democracy and the new authoritarianism in the United States. In A. H. Itwaru (Ed.), *The white supremacist state: Eurocentrism, imperialism, colonialism, racism* (pp. 157–184). Toronto: Other Eye.

Habermas, J. (1998). Modernity—An incomplete project. In H. Foster (Ed.), *The anti-aesthetic: essays on postmodern culture* (pp. 1–15). New York: The New Press.

Hall, S. (2007). The global, the local, and the return of ethnicity. In S. Hall, D. Held, D. Hubert, & K. Thompson (Eds.), *Modernity: An introduction to modern societies* (pp. 623–629). Oxford: Blackwell Publishing.

Hall, S. (2000). Cultural identity and diaspora. In N. Mirzoeff (Ed.), *Diaspora and visual culture: Representing Africans and Jews* (pp. 21–33). London: Routledge.

Hall, S. (1997). Subjects in history: Making diasporic identities. In W. Lubiano (Ed.), *The house that race built: Black Americans, U.S. terrain* (pp. 280–299). New York: Pantheon Books.

Hardt, M., & Negri, A. (2000). *Empire*. Cambridge, MA: Harvard University Press.

Harris, C. (1995). Whiteness as property. In K. Crenshaw, N. Gotanda, G. Peller, & K. Thomas (Eds.), *Critical race theory: The key writings that formed the movement* (pp. 276–291). New York: The New Press.

Isin, E. F., & Wood, P. K. (1999). *Citizenship and identity*. London: SagePublications.

Jameson, F. (2005). *Postmodernism or the cultural logic of late capitalism*. Durham: Duke University Press.

Kincheloe, J. (2005). Critical ontology and auto/biography: Being a teacher, developing a reflective teacher persona. In W. M. Roth (Ed.), *Auto/biography and auto/ethnography: Praxis of research method* (pp. 155–174). Rotterdam: Sense Publishers.

Kincheloe, J., & Steinberg, S. (2008). Indigenous knowledges in education: Complexities, dangers and profound benefits. In N. K. Denzin, Y. S. Lincoln, & L. T. Smith (Eds.), *Handbook of critical and indigenous methodologies* (pp. 135–156). Los Angeles: Sage Publications.

Ladson-Billings, G. (2000). Racialized discourses and ethnic epistemologies. In N. K. Denzin & Y. S. Lincoln (Eds.), *Handbook of qualitative research* (pp. 257–277). Thousand Oaks: Sage Publications.

Pinar, W. (2000). Strange fruit: Race, sex, and an autobiography of alterity. In P. P. Trifonas (Ed.), *Revolutionary pedagogies: Cultural politics, instituting education, and the discourse of theory* (pp. 30–46). New York: Routledge Falmer.

Pinar, W. (1994). *Auto/biography, politics, and sexuality: Essays in curriculum theory, 1972–1992*. New York: Peter Lang.

Reed-Danahay, D. E. (1997). Introduction. In D. E. Reed-Danahay (Ed.), *Auto/ethnography: Rewriting the self and the social* (pp. 1–17). Oxford: Berg.

Richardson, L. (2000). Writing: A method of inquiry. In N. K. Denzin, & Y. S. Lincoln (Eds.), *Handbook of qualitative research* (pp. 923–948). Thousand Oaks, CA: Sage.

Roth, W. M. (2005). *Auto/biography and auto/ethnography: Praxis of research method*. Rotterdam: Sense Publishers.

Scott, D. (1995). Colonial governmentality. *Social Text, 43,* 191–220.
Wolcott, H. F. (2004). The ethnographic autobiography. *Auto/Biography, 12*(2), 93–106.
Wynter, S. (1995). The pope must have been drunk, the king of castile a madman: Culture as actuality, and the Caribbean rethinking modernity. In A. Rupercht & C. Taiana (Eds.), *The reordering of culture: Latin America, the Caribbean and Canada (in the hood)* (pp. 1–41). Ottawa: Carleton University Press.

4.

Diaspora, Citizenry, Becoming Human, and the Education of African Canadian Youth

The unceasing emergence of transnational and multicultural identities in Canada has raised important questions with regard to how the politics of race, citizenry, and Diaspora play out in educational institutions. This chapter works to interrupt colonial epistemological configurations of citizenry as historically institutionalized through the conduits of schooling and education. In doing so, I query the ways in which African Canadian youth come to understand questions of citizenry and what it means to be human through ancestral familyhood, belief in a common origin, shared histories, and collective consciousness immanent to the African Diaspora. I am concerned with the lived experiences of African Canadian youth regarding questions of the self, as the self comes to be historically contoured through the social terrain of the immutable cultural constellations of Euro-modernity. I am interested in how and by what means African Canadian Diasporized people come to make meaning of their everyday social interactions. By way of critical social theory, the pedagogical hope is to invoke a sense of critical perspicacity on the quotidian moments within Diasporic life in order to understand how the myriad experiences of African Canadian youth might come to be accepted through colonial forms of abjection. Moreover, it is important to understand how abjection as immanent to colonialism embodies the ethical and moral conditions of Diasporic "truths" for African Canadian youth to come to make meaning of their experiences within the governing socio-cultural environments in which they reside. Through this interpretive framework, I write to make sense of the way in which terms of citizenry, belonging, and race necessitate and constitute each other. In particular, I wish to explore how citizenry and belonging are spatiotemporally shifting concepts, contested and historically implicating how African Canadian youth experience civic participation in the globalized context of the nation-state. The purpose here is to extricate the category of "African Canadian youth" from a homogenous socialization of historical, hegemonic Eurocentric cultural practices of modernity by engaging in what I understand to be "selective communicative practices" that come to self-determine civic participation of African Canadian youth within the Canadian public sphere. In other words, I am concerned here with how African Canadian youth come to make intelligible belonging to place through a range of cultural practices and attachments involving local histories within the globalized nation-state context of Canada. In particular, the discussion is interested in the myriad historical orientations of belonging for African Canadian youth as belonging becomes socially constructed and discursively produced within contemporary Canadian societies.

Citizenry, Coloniality, and the Emergence of the Human

Historically, citizenry in the context of Canada emerged from colonial settler nation-state relations. Yet, in coming to understand this question of citizenry as immanent to African Canadian youth, we ought to spatiotemporally locate the discursive of citizenry through particular geo-historic specificities as embodied through difference. In so doing, we allow for the variant possibilities of coming to know how questions of belonging and situatedness by way of cultural attachments come to be contextually ascribed through place to particular African Canadians. Indeed, how citizenry comes to be located in the West in relation to Africa has quite distinct moments. For the most part in the West, in particular Canada, citizenry as legitimized by the nation-state reveals itself through particular civic tropes, in which citizenry becomes imbued through universalized classification of morals and principles of equality and character, culminating in human rights and state-endowed rituals of governance (Breton, 2005; Chatterjee, 1993; Montgomery, 2005; Rose, 2007). Often enough, these said rituals of citizenry present themselves as de-raced or de-ethnicized, neutral and objective, as internalized within the imaginary of the public sphere, and as being natural to the lived experiences of what it means to be human. Yet, these naturalized rituals of citizenry have been fashioned through a constellation of historical socio-cultural elements as constituted through colonial epistemologies, which, through time and space, have concretized into an arrangement of edifices that come to be interpreted as always already permanent (Guba & Lincoln, 1994). However, concerning the human in the context of African Canadian peoples, we ought to consider how citizenry reveals itself through the myriad lived contingencies of the African Diaspora as augured through colonization, oral histories, cultural ways of knowing, Indigenous knowledge, local languages, religions, land, ancestral lineage, and spirituality (wa Thiong'o, 1986, 1993). We ought to consider how these African contingencies, when colonially uprooted by way of transatlantic enslavement, become integrated or alienated within the globalized transnational epoch of Canada, tacitly producing the conditions of possibility for African Canadian humanness.

Notable and central to the performative practices of citizenry in the context of Canada are the agentizing acts of being human as cryptically scripted through Enlightenment narratives of Euromodernity, which have historically been made possible through particular historical exigencies, such as hypermilitarized forms of violence, expropriation of Indigenous lands, and Indentureship and enslavement of African peoples. The utopian objective has been the formation of the liberal democratic state, in which, historically, citizenry, for the preferred subject, has been represented through the cultural logic of the colonial settler (see also Jameson, 2005). Ultimately, this historical cultural logic of the colonial settler gave rise to a particular citizenry as formed through a cultural homogeneity immanent to the Eurocentric West. This cultural logic was supposedly objective, and universalized as ontological, as some natural process. At the same time, citizenry as emerging from the African Diaspora through anti-colonial practices by way of transatlantic movement becomes immersed within a host of hegemonic cultural exchanges of Western modernity. These cultural exchanges, through the advent of time and myriad configurations of globalization, become spatially located, simultaneously ascribing political articulations of citizenry and agency onto African Canadian youth. Within the contemporary epoch of late modernity, these political articulations of African Canadian citizenry diverge and converge through discontinuities and continuities of primordial encryptions of belonging to a particular place, that of Africa, as well as being contiguous with the governing cultural edicts of what it means to belong within the nation-state of Canada. For citizenry of the "Other"—historicized as being less than human, inferior to Western culture, and abject (Fanon, 1963, 1967)—to come into the human condition involves taking up practices, attitudes, expressions, dispositions of Western culture as one's own (Bourdieu, 1991). This simultaneously promotes the understanding and the acceptance of the local culture of the "Other" as inferior, hence strategically distancing the self in ways in which one has to de-race, de-ethnicize, and de-culturalize the self to come into the freedoms of what it means to be human.

Of interest is the relationship with these different forms of citizenry as they come to coalesce within the Western sphere, and as they shape and reshape the historical contours of the Western subject. What are the challenges of invoking a sum secured identity onto African Canadian youth, as this sense of being secured comes to be troubled through complex Diasporized histories? What are the limits and possibilities of being human by way of coming to belong to a particular Diasporized nationalist identity through protean yet immutable classificatory edifices, such as race, sexuality, gender, language, religion, ethnicity, nationalism, ableism, and culture? How might we understand variant African Canadian youth subjectivities as experienced through situational boundaries, contingent events within the interstices of nation-state Canada, and cultural practices immanent to the African Diaspora? How do we make sense of the ways in which African Canadian youth come to be situated? At the same time, how do African Canadian youth stabilize different political identities through particular historical paradigms?

Admittedly, this involves some arduous work. It involves thinking about what it means to have an invested interest in African Canadian youth, about the social science research methods we utilize within the educational context of African Canadian youth to engage in this arduous work, and in doing so, what particular political identities are challenged, secured, made privileged, and empowered. I imagine it involves historically charting the colonial project of education and implicating the role of archetype expert texts in fragmenting the world into "us," "them," and "Other" schisms, and hence the constructing of particular privileged and simultaneous disenfranchised geographies. It involves questions of collective responsibility for pedagogues with the aim of social change, social justice, and lifelong learning. This is an invitation to understand the citizenry of African Canadian as an embodied discursive material space, which comes to be constituted through particular historical practices. It is a material space that becomes shaped through the continuities and discontinuities of the primordial (Geertz, 1983) and simultaneously through socio-cultural contingent discourses. The challenge, as Gramsci (1971) reminds us, is to come to know subjectivity through the historically specific procedures that have tacitly sedimented limitless traits within the self. How then do we understand African Canadianness through ancestral familyhood, belief in a common origin, shared histories, and collective consciousness as transatlantically relocated, spatiotemporally reconfigured, and socio-culturally constituted practices? I ask this, keeping in mind that Diasporized folks who historically have embodied social spaces since the colonization of time (Smith, 1999) have provided alternative possibilities for different African people to come to de-centre the colonial unified subject (Hall, 1997, 2000, 2005).

Belonging, Being Human, and Questions of the Primordial

With the African Diaspora procuring different geo-locations for African Canadian peoples, belonging then becomes experienced through memory of the colonial past and present, and through an embodiment of knowledge as ontologically embedded within cultural artifacts, practices, and variant attachments to the African Diaspora. It is about memory of the past and present. Belonging for African Canadian youth becomes contingent on a multiplicity of factors productive of modes of inclusion and exclusion. We need to think about the means of inclusion and exclusion that govern the lived, the sociocultural public sphere of African Canadian youth. We need to dialectically place the communities of African Canadian youth in relation to colonialism, settler nation-state, Eurocentric immigration policies, and anti-colonial practices to historically trace the socio-cultural regulation of African Canadian communities as inscribed through the colonial forays embedded within imperial immigration policies. Importantly, African Canadian youth, through the historical contours of capitalism, Diaspora, Civil Rights, and anti-colonial interventions, have come to diverge and converge in ways that are multi-ethnic, multilingual, and multifaith. Heterogeneous, to say the least, African Canadian youth are transhistorically buttressed in the present neo-liberal nation-state that is deployed as multicultural. What I am primarily concerned with now regarding African Canadian youth are contemporary questions of governance by way of particular sociocultural practices that come to inform everyday communicative exchanges. What are the ways in which the lived, socio-cultural practices of African Canadian youth become governed through primordial routes as historically imbued through the shared collective consciousness of the African Diaspora? Notably, primordial intersubjectivities of African Canadian youth are protean, existing within the present through historical epistemes, unremittingly transformed through intergenerations of culture (see also Allahar, 1994), and continuously informing African Canadian lived experiences through inexpressible ways of coming to know and to understand their everyday, sociocultural environment. Further, I am suggesting that primordial intersubjectivities, as constituted through the African Diaspora, in and of itself, are immanent within subversive pedagogies. This lends to different forms of agency that speak to the necessity for self-determination for African Canadian youth, insofar as self-determination has become a principled factor in the quest for African peoples with historical proximities to colonial encumbering of what it means to be human.

How do we understand belonging and becoming human through shared histories, common origins, and collective consciousness immanent to the African Diaspora for Canadian youth in the present context of globalization, transnationalism within the deployed multicultural nation-state? And how do these understandings of belonging and being human come to help with providing an interpretive framework for the education of African Canadian youth? I suggest this would involve a series of transhistorical loci of questions that dialogue with historical artifacts such as colonization, migration, religion, language, and culture as these historical artifacts become spatiotemporally governed through histories of the past and present alike. The learning objective is to recognize certain instants, germane to the education of African Canadian youth, that surfaced through historic, specific interstices as cryptically codified through the different socio-cultural practices buttressed within the African Diaspora. It involves understanding the historical procedures that come to govern illiberal nomenclatures within the liberal multicultural nation-state. We ought to also understand how these different moments of African Canadian history are interconnected through shared spaces of resistance, alienation, and solidarity, and through cogent ways of integrating within contemporary society. Consequently, our epistemological challenge is to come into ways of knowing and understanding the said preconditions of African Canadian youth in which these shared transatlantic spaces of resistance, solidarity, and cogent integrative practices come to be constituted and govern the self within the present epoch. Importantly, these cultural, transatlantic lacunae of the African Diaspora, as constituted between the primordial and the present, the material and the immaterial, ought to be reified to hence understand transformative possibilities for the education of African Canadian youth.

With the education of African Canadian youth, it is important to note African Canadian subjectivities as shaped through cultural Diasporized sensibilities, and how and what self-determining communicative practices become governed through embodied transatlantic temporalities. Yet, these transatlantic cultural subjectivities of African Canadian youth, as spatially located through the primordial and the present, invariably parlay themselves through mutually exclusive cultural practices within the governing public sphere, and, at times, are dependent on each other coexisting harmoniously. On occasion, these transatlantic subjectivities of African Canadian youth articulate themselves in varied tendencies without unevenness; yet simultaneously they operationalize tangentially or even counter to the hegemonic cultural politics immanent to nation-state citizenry. This hermeneutic task, in and of itself, becomes an exercise in decolonization as it accords de-centering hegemonic ways of knowing. However, decolonization for purposes of self-determination of African Canadian youth involves dialoguing with local knowledge (Geertz, 1983), local knowledge as imbued through Diasporized polities and cultural sensibilities. Also, self-determination for African Canadian youth, as transhistorically augured, comes into the human through particular terms and conditions of the governing neo-liberal public sphere. Hence, within the racialized particularities of the present, self-determination of African Canadian youth becomes reified through subjectivities, which dialectically interact with its quotidian sociocultural environment through variable modes of desire and affect to come into some sense of self-actualization for African-Canadian youth.

Canadian peoples become charted and mapped in tacit ways that locate the present self simultaneously within the historical simulacra of the preferred Euro-Enlightenment subject. What emerges for African Canadian peoples from these instantaneous corporeal referencing of colonial Enlightenment modernity are a series of cultural relations that cross-sectionally embed embodied modalities of what it means to belong and become human for African Canadian youth as Diasporized within the present. One of the ongoing challenges for the education of African Canadian youth is with understanding how belonging and being human are spatiotemporally governed by primordial means, and how the primordial becomes discursively produced and delimited heuristically through embodied ways of knowing, yet discursively figured through capitalist enterprise.

Citizenship, Multiculturalism, Diasporized Sensibilities, and Belonging in the Nation-State: Constraints, Regularities, and Possibilities for Becoming Human

What, then, does it mean for African Canadian youth to come to know the self through geo-histories, through their corporeality that has been historically situated as abject, as materially ontological to plantation geographies, and as dehumanized through colonial epistemologies? How do we make sense of this human immanent to this heterogeneous spatiality of African Canadian youth? Seemingly, these different geographies speak to the phenomenological modalities of Euro-modernity (Appadurai, 1996; Bauman, 2004; Foucault, 2007; Giddens, 1990, 1991; Gilroy, 1993; Goldberg, 2002; Habermas, 1998; Scott, 1995; Wynter, 1995a, 1995b, 2001). Through these geographies we are left to make sense of how African Canadian youth and nation-state simultaneously come to recognize each other. Put another way, we are left to make sense of how African Canadian youth come into the material through protean-like desires and performatives, as well as how African Canadian youth endow particular dualisms immanent to nation-state imbued citizenry, such as permanence and the temporary, finitude and infinitude, and the mutable and immutable forays of being human. To come into this humanism through citizenship would entail embodying particular values, expressions, desires, attitudes, and articulations as parlayed through the historical dispositions of Euro-modernity. These performative moments of the African subject all come to be circumscribed by the state through this classification of ethnicity. Sylvia Wynter's argument is important here, when she notes, "[T]he struggle of our new millennium will be one between the ongoing imperative of securing the well-being of our present ethnoclass (i.e., Western bourgeois) conception of the human" (Wynter, 2003: 260). Given the nation-state's historical gripe to secure homogeneity of citizenry and the African Diaspora syncretizing transhistorically through contemporaneous cultural variants, what we have through these tensions, then, are different articulations of the human becoming ontologically embodied by African Canadian youth.

James (1993) argues for the need for a nation-state to produce the integrative citizen, keeping in mind this integration has been, and continues to be, produced in and through a racialized gendering as governed through the capitalist mode of production, one that includes and simultaneously excludes racialized people of the Diaspora. Furthermore, my concern with belonging and being human is that it seems to be always already discursively positioned within spaces of the West, replete with a desire to consume the colonial harvest of globalization, and eagerly willing to be immersed within the techno-capitalist sphere of our contemporary social environment (Ahmad, 2008; Jameson, 2005; Mclaren & Farahmandpur, 2005). If we are speaking about the variegated forms of citizenry of African Canadian youth as contextualized through particular historical precedents, we ought then to note the implications and the intricacies of the ethnoracial histories of African Canadian youth, and the relationship with the state. This complex imperial relationship speaks to the spatiality of race. Space then becomes racialized/territorialized through particular historical readings on the body (McDermott & Simmons, 2013). Legitimized and naturalized belongings become located in spaces in ways in which citizenry becomes engendered through Eurocentric forms of habitus. Indeed, the materialization of space consists of certain procedural arrangements. Citizenry as historically imbued through the "historical racial schema" (Fanon, 1967) positions African Canadian youth in ways that de-settle colonial geographies while at the same time stabilizing the national subject (Ahmed, 2000; McKittrick, 2006; Scott, 1995; Simmons, 2010, 2014; Thobani, 2007). Althusser's "interpellation" is important here, particularly the thinking about how the material is engaged and the suggestion that "an ideology always exists in an apparatus, and its practice or practices, that this existence is material" (Althusser 2001, 112). With interpellation in mind, my interest concerns the variegated ways in which the African Canadian youth becomes interpellated into the human. It concerns place/space of transnational people, that is, people as identifying with the archival procedures of the state, as ritualized into the normalized, and as governing the material choices and practices of African Canadian youth.

In effect, and as Thobani (2007) notes, African Canadian youth come to be "exalted" into being, into this accepted subject of the state. Yet, these processes of exaltation are embodied through the legal classification of "immigrant," insofar as the "immigrant" has come to be represented through historical polities of racialization. Coming to know the human through this mitigated place of "immigrant" means speaking about the different people across time and space, understanding how particular geographies come to count, to be "preferred" and to be accepted, and also understanding particular relationships with North-South geographies. Ultimately, these capillary-like relations are deeply embedded within a colonial-capitalist agenda, materializing through the auspices of globalization. North–South movements of peoples have historically been, and continue to be, ushered imperially through socioeconomic relations. Being/becoming the nation-state subject of this place is discursively legitimized as Canada involves the expropriation of Indigenous lands (Churchill, 2009; Zinn, 1997). It involves movement from geographies that have been impoverished. It involves the centering of particular Euro-cultures. It involves African Canadian people of the Diaspora installing onto itself nation-state practices and policies that accord privilege, the privilege that concomitantly articulates complicity with the colonial governmentality of the state. Doing citizenry for African Canadian youth involves having relationships with the land and the state; it involves Pierre Trudeau's policy of multiculturalism, which supposedly allowed for a legal turn from the colonial perception of white Canada to an inclusive Canada, and concomitantly welcomed people of Southern geographies. What, then, does this nation-state deployed discursive of multiculturalism mean for African Canadian youth within present-day forms of citizenry in the context of post-Trudeau Canada? Although promising, multiculturalism as a legal policy represented many limitations concerning questions addressing the historical sociocultural context about citizenry, difference, and Diasporized people, systemic racism, power, and privilege. Multiculturalism, however, has given the Canadian state the agency to re-inscribe the nation through people of difference, primarily through the organization of racial and linguistic differences as these differences come to be articulated through the celebratory trope of culture (Ahmed,

2000; Brand, 2001; Ibrahim, 2000; Simmons, 2011; Thobani, 2007; Walcott, 2003). Hence, the material tensions immanent within the coloniality of nation-state come to be masked through the normatizing of Diasporic silence. Multiculturalism, then, allows for African Canadian youth to legally perform citizenry through one's subjectivity by way of accepting these standardized social practices as engendered through the nation-state. At the same time, the question of authentication always remains suspect regarding the citizenry of African Canadian youth. Belonging to a nation involves a particular discursive material production of the social. It involves social relations of production. It involves the act of African Canadian youth recognizing the ritualized dispositions of citizenry, an interpellating act that concomitantly continues to produce what it means to be human by way of centering this variegated articulation of the Euro-Enlightenment subject in relation to the abject, tangentialized subject of difference. Perhaps we also need to remind ourselves that this discursive material production of citizenry is underscored by the expropriation of Indigenous lands, the extermination of Indigenous peoples, and the colonial conquest of Indigenousness in which the axiological, the ontological, and the epistemological ways of coming to know across time and space have been deemed universally inferior in their totality (Abdi, 2011; Dei & Simmons, 2009, 2012). What multiculturalism has yet to do is own up to how these different cultures, as located through histories of conquest, come to be relocated within the imperial West, and, at the same time, how this relocation becomes constituted through the exploitation of local peoples and the underdevelopment of racialized geographies (McLaren & Farahmandpur, 2005; Rodney, 1982). If we are thinking of belonging and being human as governed through the discursivities of multiculturalism, then I am suggesting we ought to dis- entangle the politics of movement embedded within the congeries of the nation-state, globalization, and the Diaspora, inasmuch as this politics of movement is about the material as constituted through race.

Conclusion

With this discussion, I addressed particular modes of belonging and becoming human for African Canadian youth as engendered through cultural practices, attachments, and Diasporic situatedness. I am suggesting the education of African Canadian youth must consider how citizenry, as a historical variant concomitant to colonial modernity, come to imperially encumber African Canadian youth as essentialized ontological artifacts to particular geo-spaces of the African Diaspora. I am suggesting the governing culture of schooling and education ensues a particular type of citizenry, one in which the determinants have been buttressed through historical trajectories to colonization that works to produce disenfranchising humanisms for African Canadian youth, simultaneously enabling some hegemonic sense of sovereign citizenry through a host of cultural practices and attachments. Citizenry in our contemporaneous moment, as discursively formed through schooling and education, and as embedded within the governing culture of colonial modernity, unevenly organizes African Canadian youth within their socio-cultural public sphere through certain reactionary programs entitled by means of the nomenclatures of "diversity" and "equity." If we are thinking about the education of African Canadian youth, we ought to consider the ways in which African Canadian histories come to be displaced from institutionalized forms of education, in that we ought to think of education through difference, and how knowledge resides within the experience of all peoples. If our collective goal speaks to questions of social change and justice, it seems to me one of the challenges for educational delivery, especially when it comes to understanding what it means *to be* African Canadian youth in our contemporary historical moment, lies with coming to understand differently what it means *to be human*.

First published—Simmons, M. (2016). Diaspora, citizenry, becoming human, and the education of African-Canadian youth. In A. Abdi & A. Ibrahim (Eds.). *The Education of African-Canadian Children: Critical Perspectives* (pp. 58–72). Kingston: McGill-Queen's University Press.

References

Abdi, A. (2011). African philosophies of education: Deconstructing the colonial and reconstructing the Indigenous. In G. Dei (Ed.), *Indigenous philosophies and critical education: A reader* (pp. 80–91). New York: Peter Lang.

Ahmad, A. (2008). *In theory: Classes, nations, literatures*. New York: Verso.

Ahmed, S. (2000). Multiculturalism and the proximity of strangers. In S. Ahmed (Ed.), *Strange encounters: Embodied others in post-coloniality* (pp. 95–113). New York: Routledge.

Allahar, A. L. (1994). More than an Oxymoron: Ethnicity and the social construction of primordial attachment. *Canadian Ethnic Studies, 26*(3), 18–33.

Althusser, L. (2001). *Lenin and philosophy and other essays*. New York: Monthly Review Press.

Appadurai, A. (1996). *Modernity at large: Cultural dimensions of globalization*. Minneapolis: University of Minnesota Press.

Bauman, Z. (2004). *Wasted lives: Modernity and its outcasts*. Cambridge: Polity.

Bourdieu, P. (1991). *Language and symbolic power*. Cambridge, MA: Harvard University Press.

Brand, D. (2001). *A map to the door of no return: Notes to belonging*. Toronto: Random House.

Breton, R. (2005). Ethnicity and change in Canada. In R. Breton (Ed.), *Ethnic relations in Canada: Institutional dynamics* (pp. 289–324). Montreal & Kingston: McGill-Queen's University Press.

Chatterjee, P. (1993). Nationalism as a problem in the history of political ideas. In P. Chatterjee (Ed.), *Nationalist thought and the colonial world: A derivative discourse* (pp. 1–35). London: Zed Books.

Churchill, W. (2009). The Indigenous world: Struggles for traditional lands and ways of life. In A. H. Itwaru (Ed.), *The white supremacist state: Eurocentrism, imperialism, colonialism, racism* (pp. 1–24). Toronto: Other Eye.

Dei, G. J. S., & Simmons, M. (2009). The Indigenous as a site of decolonizing knowledge about conventional development and the link with education: The African case. In J. Langdon (Ed.), *Indigenous knowledges, development and education* (pp. 15–36). Rotterdam: Sense Publishers.

Dei, G. J. S., & Simmons, M. (2012). Writing diasporic indigeneity through critical research and social method. In S. Steinberg & G. Cannella (Eds.), *Critical qualitative research reader* (pp. 296–306). New York: Peter Lang.

Fanon, F. (1963). *The wretched of the earth*. New York: Grove Press.

Fanon, F. (1967). *Black skin, white masks*. New York: Grove Press.

Foucault, M. (2007). *The politics of truth*. Los Angeles: Semiotext(e).

Geertz, C. (1983). *Local knowledge: Further essays in interpretive anthropology*. New York: Basic Books.

Giddens, A. (1990). *The consequences of modernity*. California: Stanford University Press.

Giddens, A. (1991). *Modernity and self-identity: Self and society in the late modern age*. California: Stanford University Press.

Gilroy, P. (1993). *The black Atlantic: Modernity and double-consciousness*. Cambridge, MA: Harvard University Press.

Goldberg, D. T. (2002). *The racial state*. Oxford: Blackwell Publishing.

Gramsci, A. (1971). *Selections from the prison notebooks.* New York: International Publishers.

Guba, E. G., & Lincoln, Y. S. (1994). Competing paradigms in qualitative research. In N. K. Denzin & Y. S. Lincoln (Eds.), *Handbook of qualitative research* (pp. 105–117). Thousand Oaks, CA: Sage.

Habermas, J. (1998). Modernity—An incomplete project. In H. Foster (Ed.), *The anti-aesthetic: Essays on postmodern culture* (pp. 1–15). New York: The New Press.

Hall, S. (1997). Subjects in history: Making diasporic identities. In W. Lubiano (Ed.), *The house that race built: Black Americans, U.S. terrain* (pp. 280–299). New York: Pantheon Books.

Hall, S. (2000). Cultural identity and diaspora. In N. Mirzoeff (Ed.), *Diaspora and visual culture: Representing Africans and Jews* (pp. 21–33). London: Routledge.

Hall, S. (2005). New ethnicities. In D. Morley & K. Chen (Eds.), *Stuart Hall: Critical dialogues in cultural studies* (pp. 441–449). New York: Routledge.

Ibrahim, A. E. K. M. (2000). 'Hey, ain't I black too?' The politics of becoming black. In R. Walcott (Ed.), *Rude: Contemporary black Canadian cultural criticism* (pp. 109–136). Toronto: Insomniac Press.

James, C. L. R. (1993). *American civilization.* Cambridge, MA: Blackwell Publishers.

Jameson, F. (2005). *Postmodernism or the cultural logic of late capitalism.* Durham: Duke University Press.

McDermott, M., & Simmons, M. (2013). Embodiment and the spatialization of race. In G. J. S. Dei & M. Lordan (Eds.), *Contemporary issues in the sociology of race and ethnicity: A critical reader* (pp. 153–168). New York: Peter Lang.

McKittrick, K. (2006). *Demonic grounds: Black women and the cartographies of struggle.* Minneapolis: University of Minnesota Press.

Mclaren, P., & Farahmandpur, R. (2005). *Teaching against global capitalism and the new imperialism.* New York: Rowman and Littlefield Publishers.

Montgomery, K. (2005). Banal race-thinking: Ties of blood. Canadian history textbooks and ethnic nationalism. *Paedagogica Historica, 41*(3), 313–336.

Rodney, W. (1982). *How Europe underdeveloped Africa.* Washington, DC: Howard University Press.

Rose, N. (2007). *Powers of freedom: Reframing political thought.* New York: Cambridge University Press.

Scott, D. (1995). Colonial governmentality. *Social Text, 43,* 191–220.

Simmons, M. (2010). Concerning modernity, the Caribbean diaspora and embodied alienation: Dialoguing with Fanon to approach an anti-colonial politic. In G. J. S. Dei & M. Simmons (Eds.), *Fanon and education: Thinking through pedagogical possibilities* (pp. 171–189). New York: Peter Lang.

Simmons, M. (2011). The race to modernity: Understanding culture through the diasporic-self. In N. Wane, A. Kempf, & M. Simmons (Eds.), *The politics of cultural knowledge* (pp. 37–50). Rotterdam: Sense Publishers.

Simmons, M. (2014). Politics of urban-diasporized youth and possibilities for belonging. In A. Ibrahim & S. Steinberg (Eds.), *Critical youth studies reader* (pp. 195–204). New York: Peter Lang.

Smith, L. T. (1999). *Decolonizing methodologies: Research and Indigenous peoples.* London: Zed Books.

Thobani, S. (2007). *Exalted subject: Studies in the making of race and nation in Canada.* Toronto: University of Toronto Press.

Walcott, R. (2003). *Black like who? Writing black Canada.* Toronto: Insomniac Press.

wa Thiong'o, N. (1986). *Decolonising the mind: The politics of language in African literature.* Oxford: James Currey. Nairobi: EAEP. Portsmouth, NH: Heinemann.

wa Thiong'o, N. (1993). *Moving the centre: The struggle for cultural freedoms.* Oxford: James Currey. Nairobi: EAEP. Portsmouth, NH: Heinemann.

Wynter, S. (1995a). 1492: A new world view. In V. L. Hyatt & R. Nettleford (Eds.), *Race, discourse, and the origin of the Americas* (pp. 1–57). Washington, DC: Smithsonian Institute.

Wynter, S. (1995b). The Pope must have been drunk, the king of Castile a Madman: Culture as actuality, and the Caribbean rethinking modernity. In A. Rupercht & C. Taiana (Eds.), *The reordering of culture: Latin America, the Caribbean and Canada (in the Hood)* (pp. 1–41). Ottawa: Carleton University Press.

Wynter, S. (2001). Towards the sociogenic principle: Fanon, identity, the puzzle of conscious experience, and what it is like to be 'Black.' In M. F. Duran-Cogan & A. Gomez-Moriana (Eds.), *National identities and socio-political changes in Latin America* (pp. 30–66). New York: Routledge.

Wynter, S. (2003). Unsettling the coloniality of being/power/truth/freedom: Towards the human, after man, its overrepresentation – an argument. *The New Centennial Review, 3*(3), 257–337.

Zinn, H. (1997). *A people's history of the United States.* New York: New Press.

5.

The Race to Modernity: Understanding Culture through the Diasporic-Self

Introduction

In the much popularized postmodern context, race has often been framed as complex, sophisticated, and shifting, making way for the discursive ground of culture, ethnicity, and Diaspora. Needless to say, within the present globalized transnational epoch, one is faced with different questions concerning Diasporic identity (Hall, 2005, 2007a, 2007b). Yet race, culture, ethnicity, and identity are not distinct moments, rather they come to be discursively constituted, working in some protean way to form these different transnational identities. What I am interested in is the experience of Diasporic people concerning these contemporary questions of identity, as they come to be historically shaped through the social conjunctures of the many cultural formations of modernity. I am asking: How do Diasporic people come to understand their lived public space? How does race, as a way of knowing, form integrative spaces for Diasporic people? And how do Diasporic peoples build a working cultural register to strategically engage their everyday lived social? These are some of the burgeoning questions that I am thinking through as I engage in this discussion. So, in what is to follow, I will talk about race, culture, Diaspora, and identity in the context of modernity with the intention of opening up what I think are spaces to help disentangle some of these soundly hidden dominant–subordinate relations. My intention is to bring critical discernment concerning the ways in which place comes to be reified through race, keeping in mind place is always already constituted through people. In that, I would like us to think through culture to understand how colonizing spaces of Euromodernity become localized to particular Diasporic people. From the outset, let me say that the purpose of the discussion is not to challenge the way in which this category of Diaspora has been historically conceptualized, that is to say, what constitutes some valid displacement, dispersion, exile, exodus, or movement of a given people. I am more concerned with the socialization processes through different Diasporic people, to understand the communicative strategies and contemporary mannerisms, the particular modes of interaction that facilitate the everyday engagement of peoples in a new place. When I speak about Diaspora, I do not mean in a sum total way, dislocation of a people, though in some sense dislocation is what is experienced, nor am I speaking about a totalizing experience of exile, though these are all part and parcel of the Diasporic experience. In a sense then, I am not speaking about the Diaspora as a sum classifying system, while at the same time I am. Yet with working with these entangled overtones, I am more thinking of the movement of people to different geographies, a movement whereby people come to know themselves through the margins of their contemporary public sphere. I am more concerned about identity, citizenry, and the relationship with the state and in what way this sense of nationalism is approached through the Diasporization of peoples. I am less occupied with what constitutes a legitimate Diaspora, or in historically tracing the trajectory of movement of particular peoples, or why one moves to a different geography, nor will I attempt to pin down the Diaspora to a historic time frame, space, geography, or to some body. Instead, I am more speaking from my lived experiences with the intention of engaging in a self-reflexive dialogue in which Diasporic bodies can come to interpret their respective experiences.

Citizenship and Humanism

I begin in March 2008, Glossop Road, Sheffield, England. It was the designated reading week for most graduate schools in Canada. I had the opportunity to listen to a thesis defense at one of the academic institutions in Sheffield. But while in Sheffield, what got my attention was what was the popular debate in the mass media public sphere (Appadurai, 1996; Brantlinger, 1990; Fraser, 1992; Habermas, 1991). From newspapers to television, what was shoved in my face was the question of Britishness. Some of the headlines were, "What does it mean to be British? Is allegiance to the Queen enough to be British? And is Britishness, Englishness?" I was a bit taken back by these conversations, in particular the way in which the question of citizenry and what constitutes the authentic citizen were still troubling ingredients for public sphere talk. The conversations I felt were in some collective way, hooked on some fixed category of identity. In fact what was being invoked in these mass media debates was how to inject more Britishness into British. Much of the debate was centered on the question: In this globalized society how do we begin to think of what it means to be British? And is pledging allegiance to the Queen and country sufficient to produce citizenry? But for me, concerning here from Glossop road, is the question of Diasporic citizenry, insofar as how this particular form of humanism comes to be constituted in the interest of nation-state, through the surveillance of mass media public sphere (Brantlinger, 1990; Gilliom, 2005; Shapiro, 2005). My interest concerns the way in which cultural conditions form and reshape themselves through the governance of what I call Enlightened subjectivities. I am querying how this newly everyday Diasporic citizenry rewrites the cosmopolitan through these colonially imbued Enlightened subjectivities (Horkheimer & Adorno, 2002).

From Glossop road, I was experiencing Diasporic citizenry not to say forming itself as some new counterpublic (Dawson, 1995; Gregory, 1995), but Diasporic citizenry as being located in a way whereby the Diasporic-self had to conform or adapt to the particular historic colonial conditions of citizenry. So from the beginning, the Diasporic self was always already presupposed as being outside the realm of what it means to be a British citizen within the Euro-Anglo context. More so too, there was a particular push and pull activity happening, and if I can articulate this moment as being the turbulence formed when the primacy of cultural knowledges as an ontological raw resource of the African Diaspora interacts with the cultural register of modernity (Everett, 2002; Foster, 2007), allowing for a shift and at the same time stabilizing these inherently pure, singular categories of let us say British, English or Canadian. For me, Glossop road brought up some of the tensions the Diasporic-self experiences when communicating within Euromodernity. Glossop road reminded me of ways in which racialized bodies come to be discursively positioned and interpreted in conversations. Glossop road moved me to think about how the lived experiences of the Diasporic-self come to be nuanced, through some of these historic-colonial narratives. What Glossop road did was really push me to think about what it means to communicate in a public space with multiple historic specificities or multiple modernities (Habermas, 1998), Glossop road pushed me to think about the way in which difference comes to organize around, if I can say, a particular fixed singular triumphed form of origin, while at the same time being grounded to a certain historical primacy. Britishness then in a sense, as circumscribed through the colonial scripting of the body, coalesces with emerging Diasporic modernities. Central to this debate concerning Britishness is pondering whether to include or not to include, to defend or not to defend the colonial will of British modernity.

Theorizing Culture, Diaspora, and Knowledge Formation

Glossop road speaks to the ways in which not only how Diasporized people and Diasporic geographies come to be encoded and textualized but also the aestheticization of these cartographies that produced what Fanon (Fanon 1967: 11) calls the "epidermalization of inferiority," a culturally inscribed schema, which operationalizes scaffold imbued relations onto society. So we have relations being formed where culture now becomes starting points for conversations.

wa Thiong'o tells us that "culture carries the values, ethical, moral and aesthetic by which people conceptualize or see themselves and their place in history and the universe, that these values are the basis of a society's consciousness and outlook" (wa Thiong'o, 1993: 77). Diasporic culture then as formed through this particular knowledge, and as posited in overdeveloped countries cites itself in ways whereby it is always speaking in relation to colonial narratives of the past and present alike. I say past and present for there is this ongoing reshaping and rewriting of historic colonial narratives as it is experienced through the Diasporic-self. But what is this reshaping and rewriting of colonial narratives by the Diasporic-self? Is it not the capacity for the Diasporic-self to experience other ways of knowing, other values, customs, practices, and knowingly or unknowingly participate in its everydayness? More so, experiential knowledge, embodied as one's own by the Diasporic-self, might be taken up in a synchronic way, as in the now, disconnected from histories, time, and space. Or in another context, some of the experiences of the Diasporic-self might be engaged with the conscious knowing of colonial histories. For though culture can be understood through space and time, we still experience culture through its embodiment. In that, people do not operate in vacuums, they form relations, compartmentalized or bound; culture then has the capacity to traverse through these once impermeable membranes.

Incommensurable as it were, culture is very much dependent on the embodiment, which has caused all sorts of problems for contemporary debates concerning citizenry. Diasporic culture, as it reveals itself through bodies of difference, comes to converge and diverge at different moments, such that the identity of the Diasporic-self is revealed and marked in ways where meaning and experience are understood through this omnipresent historic colonial narrative. Grand and ontologized as it were, and popularized through the chosen image, the Diasporic-self is invited to participate in certain spaces through spontaneous performances in order to strategically maneuver nation-state imperatives, imperatives that more so give guidelines on how race, gender, space, and time ought to be engaged (Balibar, 2002; Collins, 2000; Goldberg, 2002). Time here though accompanies itself with this cultural register of modernity (Habermas, 1998), which continuously updates itself with particular currencies on the re-marked Diasporic-self. Importantly then for the Diasporic-self as located in the contemporary West is identifying marked spaces where the colonial aesthetic comes to reside, that is, being cognizant of the dominant encoded currency within one's governing social space. In that, the Diasporic-self becomes encoded in a way that accords mobility through the myriad inter-intra cultural relations. Difference, in a sense then, forms de-symmetric relations, operating tangential to these colonial inscribed meanings as popularized by mass media. Fluid, dynamic, transformative as it were, culture, though spatial, comes to be represented through the Diasporic-self. Culture has these transformative and mutable components, resulting in the ever transcendental Diasporic-self. Transcendental as they may be, identities are neither separated nor fixed to particular historical domains. Difference-sameness of culture, at times, is more so negotiating, or cognizant of each other's anachronistic spatio-temporal (see also Horkheimer & Adorno, 2002: 20), that is, those moments of coming to recognize or placing the different geographies of historical mannerisms and expressions on one's cultural register. So as difference emerges through multiple historical geo-domains, the Diasporic-self then comes into a social reality, where continuously meaning, as constituted through difference, transforms itself in ways that there is no fixed historical locus. But the Diasporic-self is not independent of history, that there is always already some lineage to a particular time, space and geography. On the same note, it is not that these histories are bringing a fixed homogenous reading onto the Diasporic-self, for within these histories, heterogeneity is very much central to the experiences of the Diasporic-self. What we are left with is that culture now has slowly shifted from the manner in which it was accorded currency through the Enlightenment knowledge of modernity (Foucault, 2007; Horkheimer & Adorno, 2002), not that it has disengaged with the prototypical colonial production, but it is this colonial edifice that has re-shaped and re-formed itself in order to be congruent with the neo-colonial/globalized particularities of our cultural present.

Ethnicity and Questions Concerning Cultural Resources of the Diaspora

Here in Canada, there is also this pledge of allegiance to the Queen for Canadianness. Canadianness has become a major terminal for Diasporic communities to take up the designated position of Enlightenment. But taking up the oath of allegiance has its own implications. I often think of: What does it mean for one to have come from a land that has been historically colonized to a space where one is in a position to benefit from nation-state violence, that is, how does one negotiate these unfreedoms, that of citizenry, nation-state, and Diasporic subjectivity? (Hall, 2007b; McKittrick, 2006; Walcott, 2003; Wynter, 2001). So if Diasporic subjectivities come to culminate with proximity to modernity's Enlightened subject, what does it say then for the African Diasporic community that has been historically determined through colonialism? How does the Diasporic-self that emerged from a colonized geography, one placed within the heart of the supposed Enlightened space, work with these debasing histories as a raw resource? In that, immanent to Diasporic movement, movement that ought to supposedly bring this better way of life, there is a particular performance by Diasporized people, one that attaches itself to modernity and simultaneously distancing itself from those spaces assigned as less than to colonial geographies. This lived experience of Diasporized people as determined through colonial inscribed sub-human categories and spaces has become the omnipresent reminder for African Diasporic consciousness, the omnipresent determinant for post-human relations (Weheliye, 2002). In a sense then, Diasporic people always already have to be constantly glancing back to make sure the sub-human does not catch up or is not too close. But even this glance back by Diasporic people to confirm progress is to understand that this sub-human distancing is part and parcel of the post-human. The question of injecting more Britishness into British, in a sense though, can be positioned as a determining act of coming up with different ways to inculcate this Enlightened humanism. How Britishness is taken up in the public sphere, is as if, collectively by *nature's* plan, we had a shared understanding of what is authentic Britishness. So then, if for now we can think of Britishness as historically determined through particular forms of knowledge, State formation, and legitimized violence, we can begin to problematize this singular pure authentic origin of Britishness. We can also push back with questions concerning how Britishness comes to be marked through the African Diaspora.

Yet, within our governing epoch, ethnicity has come to be discursively deployed in a way that works to situate, and at the same time stabilize, the Diasporic-self through particular historical conjunctures. What then does it mean to talk about the British as being ethnic? If then, from the racialized "Other" to the Black spatio-temporal, one is forever ethnic, what then are the constitutive determinants of ethnicity? Let us for the moment think through the discourse of Canadianness to understand the loci of particular people, and think about what it means to be Canadian in the context of nation-state, Diaspora, and transnationalism (Appadurai, 1996; Walcott, 2003), think about the historical social formations and the ensuing trope of being Canadian as contextualized through the interstices of ethnicity. Where then are the spaces for Black Diaspora, spaces that have come to be written out of the institutionalized text? What I am struggling with is the manner in which the discourse of difference, and at the same time the discourse of ethnicity, comes to be invoked within the civic sphere of public life. From the dominant location, from State to media, ethnicity extends across the horizon of the Diasporized "Other" to those outside the construct of Britishness (Hall, 2007a). But within black geographies there is talk about ethnicity from the dominant position, but also within Blackness there is talk about difference from within, which I think, at times, could be troubling, that there is a particular danger we need to tease out, in that, historically, alterity as a material good, as embedded through time, through particular social categories, worked to organize the conditions for colonial relations. In the contemporary setting of the West, these colonial relations very much languish in everyday conversations concerning identity, difference, and "Other." As these conversations come to be discursively framed and represented through particular media images and different locations of ethnicity, there exists this localized mobility within the discursive terrain of the Diasporized "Other." Let us for the moment think about Blackness as homogenously conceptualized through hegemonic relations of Canadianness, let us for the moment think about Blackness as a fixed reducing reading on a particular body that has been rooted historically to colonization, that this reading forms the conditions of existence, that this reading forms the conditions of limitations and possibility for the Diasporized-body. We also need to talk about the body as geography as well, to consider how the archipelago that we come to know as the Caribbean, comes to be determined through different people lumped as the "Other." What are the implications for Diasporic people who are located in the Caribbean and co-determined through this historical collective conjuncture of ethnicity? The question of Backness has discursively moved from the Negro of plantation life to the contemporary people of color, to the politically correct racialized minoritized, the African Canadian, the African American, and Black British. Inserting self into the ethnic terrain is the brown discursive, becoming particularly vibrant within the North American context, though for the most part in Britain, the Black discursive has historically engulfed the body of the "Other," be it Asian, South-Asian, African, or Moslem. Given then the different histories that are spatially steeped in colonialism and shared dialogues of resistance, what is the experience of resistance when, let us say, in the context of the West, the mobilization of racialized peoples comes through particular moments, such that these shared experiences of colonial histories separate itself as distinct or singular moments within the classification of the "Other?" What then are the consequences for the different voices of the oppressed when the politics of identification and the politics of ethnicity work to dissipate the voice of shared colonial histories? How might we speak about ethnicity, difference, and culture, and not dilute the responsibility of speaking about racism? At the same time, we need to speak about ethnic difference beyond the racialized "Other," to include the dominant body as ethnic, to ask new questions concerning power and privilege (Hall, 2000). Ultimately, these questions reside along the lines of citizenry, nation-state representation, and the contingencies of globalization.

Mass Media Surveillance of the Diaspora

Concerning the flotsam of modernity, the question that continues itself here is that: How do we dialogue with each other and come to understand different ways of knowing in order to move beyond tolerance or a practiced partitioned form of respect? Yet as the African Diaspora moves toward emancipating its public sphere realities (Everett, 2002; Gregory, 1995), communicating then calls for the ability to read the governing domain of statements, that is, the mutable yet fixed regulating group of statements that circumscribe the body. So understanding space here is important, for it is not as if these bodies come to know themselves or come to form relations in a vacuum. The public sphere has this temporality of socio-historic specific constituents that come to mark identity, that come to give one's way of knowing, that is, our communicating capacities thrust and direction. Be it Britishness or Canadianness, I think African Diasporic communities are surveilled (Gilliom, 2005; Shapiro, 2005), not only by the State but also by self, from within the local communities. See, the glance back by the Diasporic-self allows one to be aware of the previous sub-human experience, an awareness that culminates in this constant inventory check on life structures from earlier geo-historical settings. So the aligning and distancing of each other within the African Diaspora come to be nuanced in ways that might not necessarily fragment Diasporic communities in a sum totalizing way because yes, there exist heterogeneity, that the Diaspora is constituted through different people, different identities, different experiences. What I am pushing for is that if we are talking about the African Diaspora, then we ought to acknowledge shared histories of enslavement and a particular shared racial experience, so this is not some prescription for some homogenous or fixed experience, but more so I am saying that the aligning and distancing which situate itself through Diasporic exchanges work to bring a particular tangentiality within local Diasporic relations. But it seems to me, as I locate myself as a person of the Diaspora, that this knowledge production through the everyday surveillance of that which comes to be designated as sub-humanism, that the particular way in which this knowledge comes to govern the lived Diasporic experience, lend to mark spaces of freedom and unfreedom for Diasporic people. So what happens here is that the discursive project of modernity becomes propertized by local Diasporic communities, be it intentional or not, when Diasporic people come to distance or align themselves with each other, this interaction works to re-write the discourse of what it means to be this Enlightened subject. For me, it seems like I can never extricate myself from the Fanon question: How do we extricate ourselves? (Fanon, 1967: 10).

With the need for Diasporic people to constantly have to glance back, I think it is not only about Diasporic people attempting to stay ahead of plantation life, I think it is also about the everyday question of what to retrieve from the past, more so too is the sense of how one's daily Diasporic journey comes into some sort of dialogue with this omnipresent flotsam of plantation life, that is, being conversant with cultural artifacts and expressions as a particularized way of life and as historically determined through plantation procedures. What comes up here is the question: What are the ways in which plantation life reveals itself today in this Diasporic contemporary, where disenfranchisement has reconfigured itself within contemporary globalized geographies through everyday spaces of freedom and unfreedom? Also, as these everyday spaces of freedom and unfreedom come to mark the determining limits of Diasporic social interaction, the challenge here then is in utilizing these same said limits to transform the Diasporic-self and at the same time not be bound to some colonial pre-configuration of the Diasporic subject. What I have experienced, in a sense, is through remembrance I have always had this longing for home beyond the physicality of some fixed geographic location. I have had to find ways in which to inscribe my everyday social space, or let us say introduce particular modes, ways of communicating within Diasporic public sphere life (Appadurai, 1996), where I can still center my experiences through which I come to know myself. With this in mind, I am thinking more of enunciation, diction as it emerged from plantation life as an Indigenous sensibility, where I think in a very strategic way, enunciation comes to be a tool for communicating through Diasporic public sphere life, Diasporic life which has been burdened with histories entangled in colonial violence, through, let us say, the dominant/subordinated coordinates of Enlightenment. But what is this Enlightenment and modernity that so many scholars have dwelled on? Understanding these classifications is a continuous process. One of my interests is trying to understand the experience of the African Diaspora, through the variable social approaches toward modernity as it plays out within the social reality of the Western cosmopolitan. But for the moment I want to think through some of the intertextual experiences concerning modernity and the Enlightenment.

Modernity and the Governance of Enlightened Subjectivities

So Foucault refers to the Enlightenment as

> An event, or a set of events and complex historical processes, that is located at a certain point in the development of European societies. As such, it includes elements of social transformation, types of political institutions, forms of knowledge, projects of rationalization of knowledge and practices, technological mutations that are very difficult to sum up in a word …. (Foucault, 2007:111).

He also talks about the attitude of modernity:

> Modernity is often spoken of as an epoch, or at least as a set of features characteristic of an epoch; situated on a calendar, it would be preceded by a more or less naïve or archaic premodernity, and followed by an enigmatic and troubling "postmodernity." And then we find ourselves asking whether modernity constitutes the sequel to the Enlightenment and its development, or whether we are to see it as a rupture or a deviation with respect to the basic principles of the eighteenth century (Foucault, 2007: 105).

For me, presently the local public sphere is that of Toronto. At the moment it is scripted as cosmopolitan, officially categorized as multicultural by the State. But if Foucault positions the Enlightenment as the "set of events and historical processes located at certain points in the development of European societies," I then would like to mark these moments to think about formations and transformations of enslavement, Indentureship, plantation life, the archipelago known as the Caribbean and let us say, the historic monstrosity of a relationship formed through

Africa, the supposed New World, and the Anglo-Euro continents. I am more interested in forms of thinking, that is: How do Diasporic people historically determined through colonialism come to make sense of their lived reality? I am more interested in how the myriad cultural expressions come to be embodied differently in order to negotiate the newness of Diasporic realities. And how is communicating within the Diasporic public sphere vectored through this vestigial memory of colonization? (Hall, 2007b; Appadurai, 1996). Concerning here too, is how this vestigial memory of colonization comes to be this ubiquitous signpost of Diasporic freedoms and unfreedoms. It is almost another form of electronic surveillance, instead more so too, the surveillance itself becomes self-regulated in and through the said Diasporic-self. What comes out of this relationship, is this regulation of cultural memory, a type of governance imbued specifically through the Diasporic cultural register. With this Diasporic cultural register, much needed here, is familiarity with the cultural discourse in practice within the contemporaneous public sphere life, only then can one take up a strategic position of communicating. With Diasporic people forming strategic positions of communicating, what ought to be understood is to say how cultural currency circulates through particular power-knowledge points, that is in an overarching way through race, language, gender and sexuality, and ableism, and also, how these categories come to be positioned by particular structures and institutions in framing the popular discourse of public sphere talk.

Aligning and distancing from Europe and plantation life by Diasporic people as a form of resistance and survival is very much real. I mean we could talk about people not being appreciative of their Diasporic Indigenous culture, or thinking their Diasporic culture as less than, that it warrants a shift away from the minoritized cultural space, or we could talk about the recognition by particular groups of their cultural currency and the strategic investments within this cultural space. See, what happens here is that Diasporic culture in a sense becomes commodified/marketized, and mobilized within this popularized cultural space allowing for what I am calling, communities of compartmentalized solidarity. So if for the moment we were to think of this public sphere space as the property of modernity's Enlightened subject where difference comes to coalesce through collective histories and shared experiences, we could then understand the way in which plantation governmentalities (Scott, 1995) play out in present-day experiences of African Diasporic people. We could more or less think of the mutability of plantocracy governance within the Diasporic public sphere in order to understand how the social transformation of Diasporic people come to organize and mobilize their everyday social reality through the limitations of these same said historically determined plantation governmentalities.

Another interest of mine is to think of modernity through the governing historical process of plantation enslavement in relation to the development of European societies, in particular, the subject formation as located to the geographies of freedom and unfreedom, and also the implications here with that of nation-state, nationalism, belonging, and citizenry in this neo-colonial globalized epoch. So to return to Glossop Road, to the mass media debate over the question of Britishness, I think what was absent with public sphere talk here were the delimiting historical determinants where race formed the constitutive elements of this geography of freedom which we come to know as English. Culture, as it reshapes itself through Diasporic relations, has very much rewritten the national discursive. In the past, to think of being British, English, or Canadian would have conjured up Anglo-Euro images. But globalization and the ensuing transnational currents have shifted the cosmopolitan schema thereby troubling Euro-modernity nation-state discourse. Yet, I am more concerned with the forms of thinking immanent to Diasporic communities when it comes to culture, and how this thinking becomes the raw resource to make meaning and engage public sphere dialogue. With Glossop road, no longer is there this one authentic "Truth" citizenry constituting a nation-state. Instead what we have are multiple subjectivities, which in and of itself work to contest this imperial nation-state narrative. But how does this play out in a mass media public sphere where what it means to be British always already ought to propagate the dominant narrative of Euro-modernity? If we think about belonging, then this brings a host of problems for Diasporic communities, for in relation to the historic nation state-discourse, we find a counter-public citizenry discursively forming itself, resulting more so in the transformation of what it means to be let us say be this British or Canadian.

Yet, implicit in the question of what it means to be British is this homogenous orientation to the cryptic script of nation-state citizenry. To belong then for the Diasporic-self means to take up particular codes as endowed through Euro-modernity and perform them as one's own. But there is a complexity here for the Diasporic-self, in that, culture and self are continuously transforming. This is not to say that the Diasporic-self can choose cultural closure, for even in this closed state culture has already reshaped itself as governed by that space and time. How then does the Diasporic-self come to negotiate with the culture of modernity and simultaneously negotiate with the culture of Diasporic Indigenous history? This is a bit complex here, that is teasing out the intersections and points of departure of these cultural spaces. I think very much here it is important to have a conversation about modernity and the Enlightenment in relation to enslavement, plantation life, and the Diasporic movement, in a sense, to understand the historical processes which constitute the "Other" as sub-human and at the same time transforming Anglo-Euro geographies into what we come to know as the human. If presupposed to the Diaspora is social transformation, then Diasporic cultural knowledge, be it counterpublic or not, ought to inform this debate of Britishness. But the national narrative concerning the British citizenry is very much informed through the nation-state discursive formations (Hall, 2000, 2007a, 2007b). To communicate one's sense of citizenry, of what it means to belong to a particular time and place within the mass media public sphere, is more so vectored through Anglo-Euro modernity's discursive search for this subject of Enlightenment. What then is the place for Diasporic cultural knowledge in rewriting its own citizenry, on its own terms within the governing mass media public sphere spaces? And how can this counterpublic cultural knowledging work to invoke a sense of being human for Diasporic people within contemporary cosmopolitan tropes of nation-state?

If we are thinking of social transformation here, then from a knowledging position Diasporic culture as an important raw resource more or less ruptures modernity's Enlightenment. So when Foucault asks if "modernity is the sequel to Enlightenment," as mentioned before, I am understanding this as part and parcel of each other, as constitutive, as operating in a continuum, whereby this Diasporic cultural knowledging brings the much-needed, what Foucault calls "deviations with respect to the basic principles of the eighteenth century" (Foucault, 2007: 105). Much of this basic eighteenth-century principles relied on the "stitching together of Scientific positivism and the development of States" (Foucault, 2007: 50). Here, with this relationship between Scientific positivism and the State, I am pondering how through this relationship the Enlightened subject was rationalized into being, that is, how is it that positivism and the State organizing procedures come to formulate what it means to be human? And how this understanding of the human legitimized the inscription of particular bodies as this universal citizen?

Permanence and Flux: The Ebb of Transnational Culture

As Diasporic culture continues to shift and reshape itself, and as it moves through the time and space of the West, I think there is this constant negotiation with self, that is, the Diasporic-self constantly asks what historic ways of life, aesthetic forms, expressions, diction, food, and music to name some, could come to provide some form of currency to take up the challenges of communicating within this governing mass media public sphere. For some Diasporic peoples, culture as it emerged from colonized Indigenous lands was knowingly forgotten; moreover, it was an act of forgetting which really ought to usher in Enlightened subjectivities. Instead what was utilized, as a substitute, was the Enlightenment culture of modernity. For some Diasporic people, it was important to not only maintain their culture but to actively pursue the Diasporic Indigenous ways of doing things, a manner that can be interpreted as being pure, absolutist, or even close. For some people of the Diaspora, much depends on the flux of the present, that is, culture as it forms itself today and differs the next day, wherein one can decide, to say choose which form of expression to take up as one's own. Regarding this choice, I think what is coming out of these geo-positions that situate themselves within Diasporic communities, is the need for a strategic engagement of their transnational globalized epoch. We can ask then: How do Diasporic people come to align themselves through the politics of culture to engage in their daily lived social? And how often does the cultural register of modernity called upon, when dialogue concerning these Diasporic raw resources, tacitly mediate conversations? The thought of Diasporic people constantly ongoing, as an everyday surveillance method, that is, the glancing back and forth to the cultural registrar of modernity is real. From cultural representations to institutionalized knowledging, to the popularized public sphere mass media discourse, we seem to at some point in time become experts in understanding how the space and time dynamics of the West come to universally culturally encode our lived reality. Indeed, the Diaspora today has brought some complexity to this cultural register of modernity. Universalized Self and "Other" classifications allowed for compartmentalized geographies of solidarity, where the phenotype of the Diasporic-self comes to be perpetually bound to particular geographic locations. Out of this classification came, what I would like to call the geo-subject, where people in a discursively totalizing way were organized and inscribed as inferior knowledge. So this omnipresent cultural register of modernity (see also Foster, 2007) now tangling with a public sphere whereby the Diaspora is not to say centered, but has shifted its locus from the margins, has to more or less, let us say, recalibrate its coordinates for difference. Imagine the difficulty here; for the Diasporic-self has fluidity, it is not, for the most part, contained in this permanent rigid category. So the way we come to know people, place, and citizenry pushes against histories of colonial singular classifications. See I think this here is the struggle at Glossop Road. And I think it concerns the relationship with knowing what it means to be British through these permanent homogenous categories of citizenry and nation-state. So it is no longer an easy check-off mark for Britishness when it comes to the cultural register of modernity. Diaspora has ushered in a cosmopolitanism where public sphere talk, be it through mass media or not, has to now take up the nuances of difference, culture, and citizenry (Habermas, 1991). Is it then, that in rekindling the debate about Britishness with questions concerning to pledge or not to pledge allegiance to the Queen, a means, or an attempt to return to a colonial, singular, pure origin of nationalism? Or is it that Diasporic communities come to form themselves as a counterpublic, more so now in a material way, seriously opening spaces for pluralism within this fabric of Englishness? This becomes a bit of a worry here, when we hear the Western world resides supposedly in the time of democracy, as trumpeted through the governing neo-liberal humanitarian discourse. Yet as the counterpublic challenges this space of freedom and unfreedom, that of Britishness, and as the cultural register of modernity discursively readjust itself to re-mark the illiberalness of Diasporic communities, I think my concern here, is with how Enlightened subjectivities come to reshape itself as it embodies the Diaspora, and how so this reshaping come to be mobilized through what were previously illiberal spaces for the Diasporic-self. So coming out of this entangled relationship with Diasporic communities and Enlightened subjects, is this sense of flux where permanent spaces of freedom and unfreedom are now reclassified, not so much by the State or mass media public sphere, but more so now by the residing Diasporic counterpublic, which materializes through its own discursive growth and finds itself now being taken up by the same mass media public sphere as their own, as always already belonging in some pure Enlightened form to the State.

Conclusion

Returning to Glossop Road, I notice as the Diasporic counterpublic tries to ensconce itself within Euro-modernity, the emerging rumble here concerns the newly reconfigured permanence and flux of what it means to be a British citizen. I think some of the problematic that the Diasporic-self is bringing, is that of: How can modernity will itself to new forms of citizenry and simultaneously secure the trope of Enlightenment? How can Britishness retain its Englishness and still allow for Diasporic communities to have a voice? The cry though to maintain allegiance to the Queen, the historical cord to Enlightenment subjectivities, I think, allows for some sense of being human, where pre-supposed, is the liberal harmony of the Enlightened subject and Diasporic communities, all in the name of continuing the will of modernity. But as the State and mass media work in tandem to secure their hold on historical formations of citizenry, and as the Diasporic counterpublic reshapes itself through cultural ways of knowing and newly found Enlightened subjectivities, what we have then is a relationship in which the colonial encodings of British citizenry come to engage the protean presence of the Diasporic-self. Materially then, what does this relationship reveal itself as? Is it that as Foucault reminds us, we need to look at those "events with complex historical process that are difficult to some up in words, those with technological mutations, those which include social transformations, those that locate themselves within political institutions, those projects of rationalization of knowledge and practices?" (Foucault, 2007: 111). So, be it Diasporic people pledging allegiance to the Queen, or as we question the classification of Britishness and Englishness, and as Diasporic communities take up their newly found place in the West, I think what Glossop Road gives us then is more so a means to question how we come to know and understand the ensuing humanism of the Diasporized-self.

First published—Simmons, M. (2011). The race to modernity: Understanding culture through the Diasporic-self. In N. Wane, A. Kempf, & M. Simmons. (Eds.). *The politics of cultural knowledge* (pp. 37–50). Rotterdam: Sense Publishers.

References

Appadurai, A. (1996). *Modernity at large: Cultural dimensions of globalization.* Minneapolis: University of Minnesota Press.
Balibar, E. (2002). The nation form: History and ideology. In E. Balibar & I. Wallerstein (Eds.), *Race, nation, class: Ambiguous identities* (pp. 86–106). New York: Verso.
Brantlinger, P. (1990). Mass culture, postmodernism, and theories of communication. In *Crusoe's footprints: Cultural studies in Britain and America* (pp. 166–198). New York: Routledge.
Collins, H. P. (2000). *Black feminist thought: Knowledge consciousness, and the politics of empowerment.* New York: Routledge.
Dawson, M. C. (1995). A black counterpublic?: Economic earthquakes, racial agenda(s), and black politics. In The Black Public Sphere Collective (Eds.), *The black public sphere: A public culture book* (pp. 199–227). Chicago: The University of Chicago Press.

Dei, G. J. S. (2006). Introduction: Mapping the terrain–Towards a new politics of resistance. In G. J. S. Dei & A. Kempf (Eds.), *Anti-colonialism and education: The politics of resistance* (pp. 1–23). Rotterdam: Sense Publishers.

Dei, G. J. S. (2008). Crash and the relevance of an anti-racism analytical lens. In G. J. S. Dei & S. S. Howard (Eds.), *Crash politics and antiracism: Interrogations of liberal race discourse* (pp. 13–23). New York: Peter Lang.

Dei, G. J. S. (2009). Afterword: The anti-colonial theory and the question of survival and responsibility. In A. Kempf (Ed.), *Breaching the colonial contract: Anti-colonialism in the US and Canada* (pp. 251–257). New York: Springer Press.

Everett, A. (2002). The revolution will be digitized: Afrocentricity and the digital public sphere. *Social Text, 20*(2 71), 125–146.

Fanon, F. (1963). *The wretched of the earth*. New York: Grove Press.

Fanon, F. (1967). *Black skin, white masks*. New York: Grove Press.

Foster, C. (2007). *Blackness & modernity: The colour of humanity and the quest for freedom*. Montreal: McGill-Queen's University Press.

Foucault, M. (2007). *The politics of truth*. LA: Semiotext(e).

Fraser, N. (1992). Rethinking the public sphere: A contribution to the critique of actually existing democracy. In C. Calhoun (Ed.), *Habermas and the public sphere*. Cambridge: MIT Press.

Gilliom, J. (2005). Resisting surveillance. *Social Text, 23*(2 83), 71–83.

Goldberg, T. D. (2002). *The racial state*. Oxford: Blackwell Publishing.

Gregory, S. (1995). Race, identity and political activism: The shifting contours of the African American public sphere. In The Black Public Sphere Collective (Eds.), *The black public sphere: A public culture book* (pp. 151–168). Chicago: The University of Chicago Press.

Habermas, J. (1991). *The structural transformation of the public sphere*. Cambridge. MIT: Press.

Habermas, J. (1998). Modernity–An incomplete project. In H. Foster (Ed.), *The anti-aesthetic: Essays on postmodern culture* (pp. 1–15). New York: The New Press.

Hall, S. (2005). New ethnicities. In D. Morley & K. Chen (Eds.), *Stuart Hall: Critical dialogues in cultural studies* (pp. 441–449). New York: Routledge.

Hall, S. (2007a). The global, the local, and the return of ethnicity. In S. Hall, D. Held, D. Hubert, & K. Thompson (Eds.), *Modernity: An introduction to modern societies* (pp. 623–629). Oxford: Blackwell Publishing.

Hall, S. (2007b). Fundamentalism, diaspora and hybridity. In S. Hall, D. Held, D. Hubert, & K. Thompson (Eds.), *Modernity: An introduction to modern societies* (pp. 629–632). Oxford: Blackwell Publishing.

Hanchard, M. (1995). Black Cinderella?: Race and the public sphere in Brazil. In The Black Public Sphere Collective (Eds.), *The black public sphere: A public culture book* (pp. 169–189). Chicago: The University of Chicago Press.

hooks, b. (1992). *Black looks: Race and representation*. Boston: South End Press.

Horkheimer, M., & Adorno, W. T. (2002). *Dialectic of enlightenment: Philosophical fragments*. California: Stanford University Press.

McKittrick, K. (2006). *Demonic grounds: Black women and the cartographies of struggle*. Minneapolis: University of Minnesota Press.

Opini, B., & Wane, N. N. (2007). When race structures "Beingness": The experiences of African Canadian women in a place they call home. In N. Massaquoi & N. Wane (Eds.), *Theorizing empowerment: Canadian perspectives on black feminist thought* (pp. 177–198). Toronto: Inanna Publications and Education.

Scott, D. (1995). Colonial governmentality. *Social Text, 43*, 191–220.

Shapiro, M. J. (2005). Every move you make: Bodies, surveillance, and media. *Social Text, 23*(2 83), 21–34.

Walcott, R. (2003). *Black like who? Writing black Canada*. Toronto: Insomniac Press.

Wane, N. N. (2006). Is decolonization possible? In G. J. S. Dei & A. Kempf (Eds.), *Anti-colonialism and education: The politics of resistance* (pp. 87–108). Rotterdam: Sense Publishers.

Wane, N. N. (2007). Canadian black feminist thought. Re-imagining new possibilities for empowerment. In N. Massoqui & N. Wane (Eds.), *Theorizing empowerment: Canadian perspectives on black feminist thought* (pp. 296–309). Toronto: Innana Publications and Education.

wa Thiong'o, N. (1993). *Moving the centre: The struggle for cultural freedoms*. Oxford: James Currey; Nairobi: EAEP; Portsmouth, NH: Heinemann.

Weheliye, A. G. (2002). Feenin: Posthuman voices in contemporary black popular music. *Social Text, 20*(2 71), 21–47.

Wynter, S. (2001). Towards the sociogenic principle: Fanon, identity, the puzzle of conscious experience, and what it is like to be "Black". In M. F. Duran-Cogan & A. Gomez-Moriana (Eds.), *National identities and socio-political changes in Latin America* (pp. 30–66). New York: Routledge.

6.

Dialogue with Fanon

Introduction

Somewhere within the humanism of Euromodernity resides the Diasporic constellation, formed through cartographies of time and space, its contours shaped through the congeries of unsettling geographies, cultural landscapes, difference, and cosmopolitanism. Diaspora, I submit, involves a co-existing constituent of the Enlightenment public sphere, one marked through transnational relations. How might we begin to understand the poetics of Diasporic life? As the title of this chapter suggests, I am concerned with how and by what means the Caribbean Diaspora come to make meaning of its everyday social interactions? Increasingly, I have been thinking about how Fanon could help me better understand this experience. Fanon too, experienced a Diasporic way of being, having moved from his place of birth, Martinique, to study clinical psychiatry in France. Arriving in Paris, in the heart of France, at the center of modernity, he bumped into racism in a particular way that was different from his Caribbean experience in Martinique. The propensity of racism as experienced in France conjured many distinct moments to his racial experience of Martinique. Being well educated, allowed his body to maneuver through, in Fanon's terms, the "historical racial schema" (Fanon, 1967: 111), as embedded in Martinique. He found that his body, as deeply entrenched within the corporeal schema of colonization, to be closer to the body of Euromodernity, proximity that brought a particular distancing to Black life as experienced in the Caribbean. In coming to France the experience taught him otherwise. How was Fanon then, in his newly found Diasporic environment to now work with this colonial human condition? What does Fanon give us by way of a decolonial turn to earnestly engage these contemporary sociomaterial enactments of race?

With this discussion, I am trying to invoke "pedagogic thoughtfulness" (Van Manen, 1997), a sense of critical discernment on day-to-day Diasporic life in order to understand how one's Diasporic experience might come to be accepted through abjection and embodied forms of alienation. The purpose here is to extricate Diasporic difference from a homogenous socialization of Euro-modernity by engaging in what I am thinking of as selective communicative practices that come to self-determine Diasporic citizenship. In what follows, I speak about hue and the way it forms itself into a material currency for the Diaspora. I am concerned with how hue comes to embody time and space. How does a particular space come to be suggestive of a certain form of hue? I am thinking about what it means for Diasporic people to have to engage these spaces through these already permanent suggestions. I bring attention to the moment whereby Diasporic people come to know, as Foster (2007) puts it, one's *ethno-racial register*. I am interested in how this ethno-racial register comes to provide *the tacit knowledge* needed to form communicative strategies that allow for temporary "extrication" from what Fanon frames as the *epidermal regions of inferiority*, that is, the locus of the Diasporic domain, what we come to know as the Caribbean. I ask some pointed questions concerning this nomenclature of the Caribbean in order to consider the historical origins and implications for the Diasporic body. I then consider the popular Black identity within the contemporary North American public sphere, that of the US Presidency, in particular some complexities concerning limitations and possibilities regarding the *fact of Blackness*. I also discuss what Fanon locates as the *alienation of Blackness*. The conversation here concerns itself with how alienation embodies the ethical and moral conditions of Diasporic "Truths." I then move to the intricacies of the Diasporic experience, through Fanon's discussion of particular acts of assimilation, integration, acculturization, and simultaneous deculturization. I am concerned here with the following question: To what extent do these acts constitute forms of strategic distancing to local Diasporic cultures? I ground the discussion by contemplating Caribbean identity, the possibilities for Diasporic intersubjectivity, the unfreedoms of becoming, and the potentiality for schooling and education.

Material Embodiment of Hue: What Is This Caribbean?

Before we set out, it is important to talk about the material conditions of Diasporic peoples, in particular, Blackness, as it constitutes the material. Also, we ought to note the relationship through enslavement and plantation life where the colonizer's epistemological imposition of hue comes to form the ontological resources for present-day "Truth" systems. We cannot discount the question of time and place, and we cannot neglect the way in which, historical meanings resonate in our daily interactions. We cannot simply trumpet the notion of democracy and say access for all regardless of ableism, race, class, gender, and sexuality. We cannot continue to talk about issues of oppression and domination through a de-raced lens that cries out to a neo-liberal humanitarian ideology. We cannot sweep the issue of hue and the co-present currency under the rug. Firstly, let me say that I am thinking of Blackness as a colonial discursive formation that organizes and inscribes particular meanings onto people as abject. I am thinking of Blackness as an already formative occasion that brings a classificatory system of "Truth" that when embodied constitutes alienation that simultaneously interpellates the Diasporic-self into its subjectivity. That, through Blackness one comes into an already disciplined way of understanding humanity.

Concerning the "already formative occasion," of Blackness, I am thinking of the ontological. Egon G. Guba and Yvonna S. Lincoln talk about ontology:

> As a reality which was shaped over time by the congeries of social, political, cultural, economic, ethnic, and gender factors, and then crystallized (reified into a series of structures that are now inappropriately) taken as "real," that is, natural and immutable. For all practical purposes the structures as "real," a virtual or historical reality. (Guba and Lincoln 1994: 110)

The ontological question then is, "what is the form and nature of reality" that governs Caribbean Diasporic people? Concerning the Caribbean, Glissant's question is important here: "What is the Caribbean in fact?" (Glissant 1999: 39). Glissant speaks about the Caribbean as being a "multiple series of relationships." Yet, immanent to these relationships are denigrating colonial constructed categories of knowledge of *Carib* and *Arawak* which come to represent Indigeousness of *Kalinago* and *Taino*. Here devalued meanings are colonially ascribed to not only a peoplehood, but in a totalizing way, to histories, geographies, time, and place, which then come to be deemed as uncivilized (Fanon 1967). I want to historically trace the origins of these colonially engendered formations to the discourse of Blackness. So, in thinking about the Caribbean through the matter of hue, my position is not a totalizing one, that is to say, that everybody that emerges from the Caribbean in a permanent way is constructed as Black, as abject. I am saying the archipelago that has come to be governed through this accepted title of *Caribbean*, was discursively organized and inscribed through grand colonial narratives. The Caribbean, or put another way, the colonial archetype for plantation life, had as its base, the material human condition of Blackness. This geography known as the *Caribbean* comes to be constituted, as Fanon would say, as *the epidermalization of inferiority*. In a sense through Euromodernity, the Caribbean was formed as this historical abject. What we ought to understand is that the Caribbean emerged through colonial Euromodernity by way of dialectic discursive fields of "whiteness/Blackness" (Goldberg 1993:43). Hence in talking about embodied Blackness, I do not think we can afford to discard the abject material embodiment immanent in Black. I think we also have to guard here against slippage in interpreting Blackness as a sum homogeneous schema of the Caribbean. So with this understanding of the Caribbean as being constituted through hue, I am thinking of hue as this shifting constitutive abject classification that endows modernity with a particular mode of orientation. I am thinking how time, place, people, and geographies, in a very totalizing way, come to be discursively scripted through hue and come to form a mode of organizing relations for Diasporic peoples. I am also mindful that within contemporary public sphere life we have no certainty that this discursive has some definite locus. Instead what is experienced is this shifting spatio-temporal terrain onto Diasporic people.

I think we ought to spend some time here and talk about the ethical and moral implications of speaking of this thing of Blackness in a way that strategically acknowledges the dominant historic classification. What are the consequences and implications, of strategically essentializing, to work with what Fanon (1967) calls "the epidermalization of inferiority," to posit this Black as abject, as denigrating? And what about essentializing? Regarding essentializing, I am thinking about the constitutive process that accords permanent negating knowledge onto Blackness. So we have to be careful here in already scripting the "limits of possibilities" onto Blackness. This is not to negate the human conditions of plantation life, that of the master-slave dialectic as void of the contemporary public. I think the question emerging here is, how do colonial moments become re-presented in our everyday lives? If we are to acknowledge this shifting spatio-temporal terrain of the Blackness, then what does it mean here to strategically essentialize? What does this mean for the Blackness to be cognizant of this designated public sphere reading of its subjectivity? What does it mean for the Black subject to understand the fluid discursive rules of Blackness? How do we extricate ourselves from Blackness? (Fanon, 1967: 10). More so, how does the Diasporic subject come to understand which discursive rule to embody and simultaneously reify as some material good? And what knowledge counts to inform everyday communicative practices, which are utilized to strategically engage the contemporary public sphere of Euro-modernity? So, if we are thinking about our contemporary public sphere, how do we understand the space of the U. S. Presidency as it emerged through Blackness?

U.S. Presidency—the Extrication of Blackness?

I remember November 4, 2008, 11–ish pm. I was glued to my computer screen, checking the elections. I do not know if I were more in shock or awe that Barack Obama won the elections. Or was it the global attention the elections received, the fact that millions were watching, listening, paying attention in some way? But what was the interest? Was it that the world was interested in political science, electoral politics, or issues pertaining to contemporary America? Or was it that Blackness won the Presidency? What about this Blackness left the world whispering? Is it that, at that moment, there was this universalized perception/understanding of, what it means to be Black? Is it that, at that moment Black was in a global way understood, as Fanon would say as the "wretched of the earth"? What does it mean then for that which is classified as the "wretched of the earth," for the body designated for plantation life, as abject to emerge to the position of presidential life? To what extent does this experience provide the conditions for "the extrication of Blackness"? Could this moment be interpreted as a moment of "ontological security"? (Giddens, 1990). And within the contemporary public sphere does ontological security work to condition pedagogic trust among difference? There was a lot of whispering about Obama's identity. American, African-American, Black, African were all tossed around. I think though, that throughout the campaign, Obama's politics became centered by way of a totalizing discourse of what it means to be an American. For example, there was a lot of debate about how Black is Obama's politics, how Obama subdued his Blackness in order to appeal and appease white voters, and how Obama denied that the election and his candidacy were about race. What are the implications here for Diasporic communities? What does it mean for "the fact of Blackness" to be part and parcel of U.S. white house operations? How does this speak to the moment Obama appeared hand in hand with the family for the token victory speech? I think we ought to talk about how we understand "the fact of Blackness" as an organizing principle of White House operations. Historically we come to know this location as organized/inscribed in and through modernity, that of presidential subjectivity. What then does this mean for modernity and the Diaspora when presidential subjectivity is now occasioned by the material of plantation life? Is this representative of this "new humanism" as Fanon spoke about? What does this moment mean for countries that have been underdeveloped? What then does it mean for imperial America to be governed by Blackness?

Alienation as a Human Condition

I want to point to what Fanon calls the "alienation of Blackness" (Fanon, 1967: 11) as a material good. I am more or less thinking about the ways in which this *alienation of Blackness* becomes the interpretive framework for Diasporic people to make meaning of its lived socioeconomic public sphere. What are some of the limits and possibilities here and, "how do we extricate ourselves?" (Fanon, 1967: 10). What are some of the communicative attitudes, desires, anxieties, and fantasies developed to mold Diasporic identity? And how is it that this "alienation of Blackness" embodies the ethical and moral conditions of "Truth," which at the same time accord certain governance on the everyday lives of Diasporic people?

In the context of the Caribbean Diaspora, *alienation of Blackness* becomes a particular experience whereby Diasporic people, through day-to-day negotiating, interact with its newly found terrain, a sort of pick and choose if you will. This is not to say this negotiating is done in some formal sense. Diasporic people go through this unyielding self-dialogue where the goal is always already to fit in or gain acceptance. One could imagine that in coming to a new place these goals would pose some challenges. I am more concerned with how and by what means, Diasporic people take up some of these challenges. With alienation as experienced from within, that is, this internalized inferiority, as a material good, as a starting point, and as alienated politically and socio-economically (Oliver, 2004), Diasporic people then as poised through what I am thinking of as a liminal constant, come to interact, come to form itself as this subjugated counterpublic, (Fraser, 1992: 123), which hereby, operates not necessarily with the will to subvert dominant spaces, but more so in a way to strategically acculturize to the existing conditions of the present public sphere. This process can become quite complex, and needless to say, problematic, for to have to discursively interface with dominant spaces, it seems to me, ensconces what Fanon speaks of as the need "to dissimulate, to deculturize and at the same time acculturize" (Fanon, 1964: 40, 41, 42). Maybe we ought to open the conversation here, to speak about dissimulation, deculturization, and acculturization, these important experiential moments for Diasporic people, what I think make for possible pedagogical moments which come to be imbued through this "alienation of Blackness."

Concerning deculturization, I am thinking of how Diasporic people, through time and space, distance themselves from continental lands, which then materializes itself through cultural modes of communicative exchange. wa Thiong'o talks about "culture as a product of a people's history, which also reflects that history and embodies a whole set of values by which people view themselves and their place in time and space" (wa Thiong'o, 1993: 42). Here, I am cognizant of the danger of bringing a particular monolith, fixed, homogenous reading of culture. By no means am I trying to peg culture to such a position. I recognize the fluidity, flux, and heterogeneity of culture. Where I am going though is to suggest that wa Thiong'o's reading is one of the possible ways of coming to understand culture and Diasporic people. If we were to think of culture as it reflects history and embodying the values of Diasporic people, we can drum up some sort of communicative discursive interface, which ought to insulate Diasporic subjectivities from governing cultural practices. Yet this discursive interface works to distance the Diasporic subject from homegrown cultural dispositions, so be it "metaphysical guilt or be it the obsession with purity" (Fanon, 1964: 18) the Diaspora then, comes to exude particular desires, anxieties, and fantasies, whereby one of the experiences as Fanon succinctly puts it, is to "judge, condemn, to abandon language, food habits, ---- way of sitting down, resting, and laughing as such" (Fanon, 1964: 39). What reveals itself in myriad ways is more of a dissimulated Diaspora where, dispositions, attitudes, expressions, and behavioral ways are specifically reshaped in order to be recognized by the popularized dominant culture. But, dissimulation requires experiential knowledge. It requires an inter-intra cultural understanding of the lived social.

Aptly, Fanon refers to this particular experiential knowledge as "technical knowledge" (Fanon, 1964). What we have with this everyday technical knowledge or as (Hook, 2006) notes, the *pre-discursive*, is in a sense a form of purposive reasoning that always already has its mode of orientation steeped within Indigeneity. It is more a mode of orientation whereby the governing locus emerges through plantation origins, which to me constitutes liminality, in that, plantation life provides for the Diaspora that consciousness, that spirit if you will, that cannot readily be felt or let us say be experienced by the dominant culture. If one of the problems being revealed here is the capacity to communicate, then we ought to remember, as Fanon reminds us, that well sketched within the Diaspora is this "historical racial schema" (Fanon, 1967: 111), a schema that comes to codify and let us say govern communicative and Diasporic interactions. If we were for the moment to think of the Diaspora as this "racial epidermal schema" then of concern here is the way in which Diasporic people become a site of cultural exchange, through which communicative practices are informed by a particular mode of reasoning, whereby one's understanding of culture becomes technical knowledge (Fanon, 1964). There is also a question of surveillance here, where hue becomes the crucible for embodied knowledge and makes possible for a re-inscribed self-regulating way of knowing for Diasporic people. As the Diaspora continues the never-ending quest for a better life in the West, and as this Diasporic life becomes more and more entrenched with the push and pull of colonial positioning, with the push and pull of Euromodernity, communicative strategies then become very important. Indigenous peoples speak about the urgent need for "survival, recovery, development and self-determination" (Smith, 1999). But how does the Diaspora take up these moments? Is it through a process of assimilation wherein the irreducible moment becomes a procedure of deracialization? What does it mean to say as a communicative pragmatic, the Diaspora, to some extent, has strategically de-raced language? To have self-determination, recovery, survival, and development be all governed in and through this particular deracialization process allows for totalizing deculturalized relations. Assimilation accords limiting conditions that obtain in a sense a permanent dismissal of Diasporic culture. If we are talking about integration then we ought to ask on whose terms. For how, then, does the public sphere of Euro modernity integrate itself with Diasporic communities and take up its multiple centers? To speak of the integration of multiple public spheres, multiple communities, and multiple centers is to be open to interactions of cultural difference.

Problems pop up when these interactions come to exist through a one-way, fixed direction, whereby the compass becomes navigated through this universalized homogeneous scripting of Euro modernity. The economic outcome is real here for the Diaspora, resulting in assimilation becoming more and more the Diasporic companion. But what ought to be taken up more than a companion-like position to Diasporic relationships is the practice of decolonization. With decolonization, Diasporic people can work with embodied ways of knowing. Diasporic people can work with the *pre-discursive*, with that experiential knowledge fecundated through local cultural resources. Importantly here, Diasporic people ought to be centered within this experience rather than being determined through some tangential existence. But what does it mean for Caribbean Diaspora to work with memories of local Indigenous histories?

Modernity, Culture, and Poetics of Diction

While in France, Fanon's Diasporic experience was influenced by the Negritude movement, which allowed him to think of "the fact of Blackness" more as a cultural Indigenous resource than as some abject source. Leopold Senghor (2001) invites us to not only think of Negritude as a form of humanism but also to think of the humanism of Negritude, in relation to the humanism as engendered through Euromodernity. He tells us that Negritude is "a will to return into oneself, that it is a will to take on the values of the Black world, to live them oneself, that one has to make descent into a series of negation to retrieve the meaning of Blackness, that Negritude is a *humanism with a universal scope*" (Senghor, 2001). But this *humanism with a universal scope*, I think, ought to be queried. Giddens (1990) asks us to think about modernity "beyond an epoch or an era, to think of modernity as an attitude, as a mode of organizing the social that emerged in Europe, to think then of modernity as a set of political, institutional, economical, cultural, social processes located at a certain point in the development of Europe that universalized its way of knowing, as knowledge for all" (Giddens, 1990, 1991). To some extent then, we are all historically determined through modernity. So when Senghor (2001) speaks of a *humanism with a universal scope*, I think too that this universality was always already discursively encoded through Eurocentric ways of knowing, and it is this discursive-material production of the *universal*, which provided the conditions of possibility and at the same time the limitations for the Negritude movement. Foucault reminds us of a certain humanism as revealed through Euromodernity which was preoccupied with a set of themes, and as preserving particular values, that was prominent in European societies (Foucault, 2007: 111). Some of these themes were racism, masculinity, femininity, sexuality, whiteness, violence, aesthetics, ableism, and religion. One of these themes that Fanon confronted was racism. A theme, in effect, that legitimized whiteness as a Eurocentric aesthetic body of knowledge, and as being the only material means to humanism. A theme, in fact, Negritude left well in place. So in a sense then, Negritude as a form of humanism was always already ethically and morally constituted through the values of the cultural register of Euromodernity. Fanon, in wanting the *wretched of the earth* to *extricate themselves from Blackness*, moved beyond the movement of Negritude. Fanon troubled the humanism of Negritude, and in doing so he centered the white-Black dialectic. That is, he asserted the location of his Blackness in relation to white, that Black was constructed in relation to white, as the abject, as that of negation. Fanon notes:

> The dialectic that brings necessity into the foundation of my freedom drives me out of myself. It shatters my unreflected position. Still in terms of consciousness, black consciousness is immanent in its own eyes. I am not a potentiality of something, I am wholly what I am. I do not have to look for the universal. No probability has any place inside me (Fanon, 1967: 135).

At the same time, Fanon challenged modernity as this Eurocentric body of knowledge, which determines this singular mode of humanism. Fanon seemed not to be convinced that Negritude was working to counter modernity as a master narrative, but more so, that Negritude thought through Euro-paradigms to retrieve and shape its cultural histories. This is not so to say in a totalizing way we ought to dismiss the project of Negritude, no. In fact, Sartre is correct when he speaks not of Negritude as anti-racist racism, but of Negritude being as a "dialectical progressive" (Sartre, 2001: 137). The question coming out here then is: to what extent did Negritude challenge or leave modernity intact as a form of humanism? Or to what extent did Negritude bring *ontological security* (Giddens, 1991: 36; 1990: 92), to Blackness?

With the colonization of time the question of modernity has been bursting. Be it a particular period, a particular epoch, be it the way of organizing life and the ensuing behavioral expressions, desires, and anxieties, be it the classification of the social. We ought to remember the historical trajectory of modernity, wherein the interests concern themselves with a particular humanity. More so, we ought to think through how this humanism has come to be universalized as a mode of knowing in our everyday life. Familiarity with this text of modernity has governed contemporary spaces, becoming in a sense, one's tacit go-to sociocultural register. Navigating through these complex and yet sophisticated contours of public sphere life could become quite challenging for Diasporic people. Given this text of modernity, what does it mean then for Diasporic people to work with a sense of home and belonging? Some have argued for a cultural supermarket, that we live in a multicultural society, where we can participate in the myriad spaces that culture offers. Choice more often comes through this selective process of understanding through embodied experiences. The cultural supermarket becomes the spatio-temporal meeting point whereby expressions, behavioral ways, and modes of thinking come to be socially organized at the site of Diasporic embodiment. The body comes to be inscribed in and through what Fanon calls the "historical racial schema" (Fanon, 1967: 111). The challenge here is to understand how Diasporic people come to be discursively scripted and simultaneously become the occasion for the "corporeal malediction" (Fanon, 1967: 111). That is, how do these socio-historical discursivities of the "corporeal schema" mold the perceptions of Diasporic spaces? How do Diasporic spaces come to be preconditioned with the interpretive faculty to make meaning of the embodiment of cultural currency? What then are some of the desires that are formed through this understanding? Where does this cultural currency reside as distinctive of its embodiment? What constitutes this cultural currency? How does the Diaspora come to know this material good of race? What are some of the socio-historic discourses that come to form this knowledge of cultural currency? And what about this thing of a Diasporic spirit? How does this Diasporic spirit come to be fecundated? What is the condition of the Diasporic spirit as it comes to be determined through these communicative exchanges?

As society becomes more and more bound through Diasporic difference, and as the determinants of modernity work to re-codify social categories, the public sphere now quickly adapts itself by reconfiguring its mode of orientation, difference that is, to the tune of Euro-modernity. So, how is it then, that Diasporic difference learns to adapt, or to what extent is Diasporic difference equipped for the challenges of the public sphere as governed through a Euro modernity mode of orientation? In a sense then, this experience begs the question of the quality of humanism within the Diaspora. Concerning the quality of humanism, Sylvia Wynter on reading Fanon, poses seemingly simple questions: "*What it is like to be human?* and *What it is like to be black?*" (Wynter, 2001: 31). We ought to note, there are different modes of the *lived experience of Blackness*, as these modes circumscribe and form constitutive elements within the constellation of the Diasporic difference. And that immanent to the "lived experience of Blackness" there is the sense of the liminal other (Wynter, 2001: 57, 58), more of an anachronistic consciousness within Diasporic difference. For the lived experience of Blackness to come into a particular humanism, to engage with "what it is like to be human," the socializing process as determined through the Diaspora, takes up different modes of organizing itself. Let us take, for instance, language and the way perceptions, desire, fantasy, behavioral patterns, culture, and communicative exchanges are shaped through this medium. For the Caribbean Diaspora, language is always already the moment of engaging with the liminality of the "self/other" (Fanon, 1967: 17: Wynter, 2001: 57, 58). It is a moment of exchange whereby Diasporic diction comes to be an appreciated/depreciated material good in which abject hue constitutes its historical base. Be it to strategically distance subjectivity from Diasporic encodings, or be it to resist the dominant culture, or be it to integrate with the dominant encodings of the Western public sphere, Diasporic diction comes into being through moments of selective performative practices. These selective practices come to circumscribe a certain experience of the peoples of the Diaspora, which Fanon amplifies when he speaks about:

> Every colonized people—in other words, every people in whose soul an inferiority complex has been created by the death and burial of its local cultural originality—finds itself face to face with the language of the civilizing nation -- (Fanon 1967: 18).

So, if we were to take language, for example, where the idealized language of the colonizer comes to be formed as the imperial sacrosanct, and to say that within the archipelago known as the Caribbean there exists a particular way in which difference is situated through diction or, if I can say through the "vernacular," I am concerned then with how language, that is, Diasporic diction comes to form itself as an archetype humanism. I want to better understand how Diasporic linguistic performatives become a disciplinary way of life, a humanism in of itself, how this performative comes to embody Diasporic culture, how this performative comes to be the identity for people of difference. I am thinking about the inter-/intra-socializing processes, that of, the communicative exchange between the Diaspora and Euromodernity and at the same time communicative exchanges through people of difference as it contains and confines itself to the geography of its Diasporic constellation. What I am left thinking about is the way in which the Caribbean Diaspora work with language as a communicative pragmatic, to cogently engage with the public sphere of Euro-modernity. To note then how this language of the Caribbean Diaspora, this language immanent to plantation life has its alterity as tangential to the paradigms of Euro-modernity?

With its Diasporic rhythms reverberating through colonized territories, Diasporic citizenry and the co-present protean come to take up this sense of a historic belonging within the framework of the nation-state. Yet, to strategically engage with this sense of belonging calls for selected communicative practices, selected communicative practices that ought to have the capacity to dialogue with this naturalized universal way of reasoning. If, then, these communicative practices are selected, how does the Diasporic subject come to understand what knowledge comes into play with this selection process? How, then do Caribbean Diasporic peoples make meaning of their lived experience in the Western public sphere? So if this sense of belonging that one takes up is entrenched colonially to subhuman status, what Fanon would call "epidermal regions of inferiority," is it then to dismiss, or maybe perhaps to rename all colonial categories? Is this part and parcel of the decolonizing project? How would this renaming project shape or rupture the Caribbean experience? Given the cultural difference, given cultural heterogeneity, what does it mean for the Diaspora in an Indigenous way to have a sense of home and belonging? Would it make for possible different discursive contours of Diasporic people? Is it that the Diaspora, in a totalizing way, as it emerged through the reservoir of plantation life, as it comes to exist, constituted through Blackness, as Euro-modernity's "other"? Fanon tells us, "it is not I (Black life) who make meaning for myself, but it is the meaning that was already there, pre-existing waiting for me" (Fanon, 1967: 134), that "I am overdetermined from without. I am the slave not of the "idea" that others have of me but of my own appearance" (Fanon, 1967: 116).

The language of the Diaspora comes to be experienced as the embodiment of its own alienation. It is not as simple to take up Fanon's ways, that is, to "extricate ourselves" or to rid ourselves of this Diasporic way of knowing and communicating. Language comes to be experienced through one's local Indigenous socio-cultural ways of coming to understand becomes silenced and it is this silence that comes to write the history of Diasporic possibilities. It is this silence that provides a platform of meaning for Diasporic experiences. If silence then becomes one of the possible modes to organize relations between the Diaspora and the public sphere of Euromodernity, how does the Diaspora come to interface with itself? How do Diasporic communities come to organize themselves, considering the inter-intra relations of cultural difference? By what means do Diasporic people as "epistemologically limited" (Gordon, 1995) through its embodied alienation engage Diasporic places by being cognizant of the proximity and distancing from its historic-cultural artifacts? How does the Diaspora come to understand the experience of the lived public, when spaces as the "town hall, institutions, school administration offices, the school, sports arenas, administrative places come to be strategic places of alienation" (Glissant, 1999: 36)?

What I am hoping to come out of this conversation is for us to bring to the surface the every day or taken-for-granted embodied "Truth" that organizes communicative principles of colonial modernity. Whether it be the morals of colonialism or colonial logic, how is this mantra taken up as one's own and, at the same time, works to position the abject Black? If, as Fanon requests, we were to de-ontologize the lived Black, then, as a starting point, we can introduce colonial historic specificities. I am more concerned here with colonial constituents, some of which are the temporal, space, violence, anachronism, dialectic of hue, racism, geographies, civilization, Euro-intelligentsia, and plantation life. Notably, there is a danger here in discarding these constituents as relic, as some irrelevant distant artifact. Instead maybe we ought to think about how these constituents come to be reshaped, and reorganize and regulate our present-day social. So as our daily conversations become mediated through these colonial constituents we can begin to wonder how certain knowledge come to be centered within different socio-cultural sites. We can come to understand what embodied knowledge is selected as a communicative procedure to form some sort of a working harmonious union. Be it a performative procedure or not, the Diasporic subject wittingly or unwittingly makes meaning through integrating viable "Truth" systems. It is not necessarily, in the sense of Fanon, that the Diasporic subject is undergoing an "inferiority complex." Rather, I think it is more about having a working understanding of the socio-economic-cultural register of modernity and how it plays out in time and space, that is, the consequences of practicing a certain reading of Diasporic people at particular social sites.

Conclusion

With this discussion, I hoped to have enhanced the potentiality for educational research by articulating the way in which Diasporised subjects come to internalize racism. I wanted to think through certain sites that operationalized the center of Fanon's colonial experience, such as race, hue, abjection, culture, and alienation. My learning objective was to bring awareness to certain discontinuities, in particular, how abject Blackness as embodied, self-regulates different Diasporic spaces. I wanted to accord cognition to Diasporic socio-historical conditions. With the hope of transforming our social reality, I wanted us to come to be critically reflexive about our experiences, in order to think about some pragmatic communicative possibilities relevant for schooling and education. In doing so, I think it is pertinent we continue to remind ourselves that this embodied alienation we are speaking about, has its mode of orientation well rooted within the interstices and aesthetics of the colonial index. As Fanon reminds us, we have a Diasporic subject then experiencing alienation of the body from within. We also have a subject here that experiences alienation from historic ways of knowing, from customs, from values, from habitual practices. There is, in a sense, an incommensurable loss (Butler, 1997; Oliver, 2004) being experienced here. I am more interested in how this sense of an incommensurable loss (Butler, 1997; Oliver, 2004), comes to seduce the Diasporic subject through a mode of thinking which brings a self-regulating surveillance that materializes itself in the production of a particular transnational subject. I am left here contemplating, how does this incommensurable loss endow the socialization process where the Diasporized subject has to integrate different socio-cognitive interests to form cogent communicative strategies of the lived social, as organized through the classificatory system of Euro-modernity? So if we were to talk about the Caribbean Diaspora, if we were to speak about Diasporic intersubjectivity and Caribbean identity, then we ought to speak about the link with colonial alienation (Oliver, 2004; Sartre, 2001). We must remember that as a starting point, and as Gordon (1995) reminds us, "ontology must be suspended"(Gordon, 1995: 14), and that the Caribbean Diaspora experiences "absolute ontological rigidity" (Gordon, 1995: 43).

What, then, are some of the pedagogical properties of this "absolute ontological rigidity," which circumscribe the everyday Diasporic experience? Is this an *absolute ontological rigidity* of race? How do we decolonize beyond the text, this illiberal *ontological rigidity* of the Diaspora?

What are the ways in which this *absolute ontological rigidity* becomes constituted through Indigeneity? How does Fanon's colonial experience diverge and converge with the contemporary Diasporic experience? By way of decolonizing pedagogies, what does Fanon offer us to subvert the homogeneity of Euromodernity's humanism? What does it mean for everyday sites of interaction, from the choice of food, to the way one speaks, to the conversation on religion that is tacitly encoded through bodies of distinct geographies, to the choice of clothes, to schooling and education, to the institutions of work, to be aesthetically and epistemologically oriented to the humanism of Euromodernity? What are the unfreedoms for the Diaspora when this humanism of Euromodernity becomes the only way out for difference? In the search for a different humanism, Fanon pushes us to think of the ontological underpinnings of our experience. Fanon leaves us pondering the form and nature of our reality: the protean elements concerning race, class, gender, sexuality, ableism, and religion, which mold and shape our existence. More so, we are left thinking about the underlying fields of knowledge that worked to conceptualize our participatory form of humanism.

We are left contemplating the ethical and moral implications of socializing through particular communicative practices. Frantz Fanon's reading of the lived experience of Blackness provides us with possible pedagogies for decolonization to understand different Diasporic experiences. Moreover, Fanon gives us the means to understand local colonial encounters and compels us to unconditionally question the colonial archetype and the immanent humanism.

First published—Simmons, M. (2010). Concerning modernity, the Caribbean Diaspora and embodied alienation: Dialoguing with Fanon to approach an anti-colonial politic. In G.J.S. Dei, & M. Simmons. (Eds.), *Fanon and education: Thinking through pedagogical possibilities* (171–189). New York: Peter Lang.

References

Bourdieu, P. (1991). *Language and symbolic power.* Cambridge, MA: Harvard University Press.

Butler, J. (1997). *The psychic life of power: Theories in subjection.* California: Stanford University Press.
Cesaire, A. (1972). *Discourse on colonialism.* New York: Monthly Review Press.
Du Bois, W. E. B. (1989). *The souls of black folk.* New York: Penguin Press.
Fanon, F. (1967). *Black skin white masks.* New York: Grove Press.
Fanon, F. (1965). *A dying colonialism.* New York: Grove Press.
Fanon, F. (1964). *Toward the African revolution.* New York: Grove Press.
Fanon, F. (1963). *The wretched of the earth.* New York: Grove Press.
Foster, C. (2007). *Blackness & modernity: The colour of humanity and the quest for freedom.* Montreal: McGill-Queen's University Press.
Foucault, M. (2007). *The politics of truth.* Los Angeles: Semiotext(e).
Foucault, M. (1995). *Discipline and punish: The birth of the prison.* New York: Vintage Books.
Fraser, N. (1992). Rethinking the public sphere: A contribution to the critique of actually existing democracy. In C. Calhoun (Ed.), *Habermas and the public sphere.* Cambridge: MIT Press.
Giddens, A. (1991). *Modernity and self-identity: Self and society in the late modern age.* California: Stanford University Press.
Giddens, A. (1990). *The consequences of modernity.* California: Stanford University Press.
Glissant, E. (1989). *Caribbean discourse: Selected essays.* Charlottesville, VA: University Press of Virginia.
Gordon, R. L. (1995). *Fanon and the crisis of European man: An essay on philosophy and the human sciences.* New York: Routledge.
Guba, E. G., & Lincoln, Y. S. (1994). Competing paradigms in qualitative research. In N. K. Denzin, & Y. S. Lincoln (Eds.), *Handbook of qualitative research* (pp. 105–117). Thousand Oaks, CA: Sage.
Habermas, J. (1991). *The structural transformation of the public sphere.* Cambridge: MIT Press.
Itwaru, A. H., & Ksonzek, N. (1994). *Closed entrances: Canadian culture and imperialism.* Toronto: TSAR.
Ladson-Billings, G. (2000). Racialized discourses and ethnic epistemologies. In N. K. Denzin & Y. S. Lincoln (Eds.), *Handbook of qualitative research* (pp. 257–277). Thousand Oaks: Sage Publications.
McKittrick, K. (2006). *Demonic grounds: Black women and the cartographies of struggle.* Minneapolis: University of Minnesota Press.
Oliver, K. (2004). *The colonization of psychic space.* Minneapolis: University of Minnesota Press.
Sartre, J.-P. (2001). Black Orpheus. In R. Bernasconi (Ed.), *Race* (pp. 115–142). Malden, MA: Blackwell Publishers.
Sekyi-Otu, A. (1996). *Fanon's dialectic of experience.* Cambridge, MA: Harvard University Press.
Senghor, L. (2001). Negritude and modernity or negritude as a humanism for the twentieth century. In R. Bernasconi (Ed.), *Race* (pp. 143–166). Malden, MA: Blackwell Publishers.

Smith, L. T. (1999). *Decolonizing methodologies: Research and indigenous peoples.* London: Zed Books & University of Otago Press.

van Manen, M. (1997). *Researching lived experience: Human science for an action sensitive pedagogy.* London, ON: The Althouse Press.

wa Thiong'o, N. (1993). *Moving the centre: The struggle for cultural freedoms.* Oxford: James Currey. Nairobi: EAEP. Portsmouth, NH: Heinemann.

wa Thiong'o, N. (1986). *Decolonising the mind: The politics of language in African literature.* Oxford: James Currey. Nairobi: EAEP. Portsmouth, NH: Heinemann.

Wynter, S. (2001). Towards the sociogenic principle: Fanon, identity, the puzzle of conscious experience, and what it is like to be "black". In M. F. Duran-Cogan & A. Gomez- Moriana (Eds.), *National identities and socio-political changes in Latin America* (pp. 30–66). New York: Routledge.

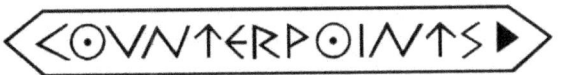

Studies in Criticality

General Editor
Shirley R. Steinberg

Counterpoints publishes the most compelling and imaginative books being written in education today. Grounded on the theoretical advances in criticalism, feminism, and postmodernism in the last two decades of the twentieth century, Counterpoints engages the meaning of these innovations in various forms of educational expression. Committed to the proposition that theoretical literature should be accessible to a variety of audiences, the series insists that its authors avoid esoteric and jargonistic languages that transform educational scholarship into an elite discourse for the initiated. Scholarly work matters only to the degree it affects consciousness and practice at multiple sites. Counterpoints' editorial policy is based on these principles and the ability of scholars to break new ground, to open new conversations, to go where educators have never gone before.

For additional information about this series or for the submission of manuscripts, please contact:

>Shirley R. Steinberg
>c/o Peter Lang Publishing, Inc.
>80 Broad Street, 5th floor
>New York, New York 10004

To order other books in this series, please contact our Customer Service Department:
>peterlang@presswarehouse.com (within the U.S.)
>orders@peterlang.com (outside the U.S.)

Or browse online by series:
>www.peterlang.com

www.ingramcontent.com/pod-product-compliance
Lightning Source LLC
Chambersburg PA
CBHW061719300426
44115CB00014B/2754